$\mathcal{T}$ABLE OF CONTENTS

INTRODUCTION

A few years ago, something happened and I was forced to realize I couldn't keep on doing what I was doing, especially the way I was doing it. I couldn't keep living a life that was so out of balance. And how did that revelation come to me? I got sick—*really sick*.

Within a few short months, I ended up having so much difficulty walking that my husband came up with the brilliant idea that I needed a wheelchair. The verdict? Multiple sclerosis—MS!

Just when I got used to the idea that I couldn't live the life I was used to, my condition got worse. My life was slipping through my fingers, like grains of sand—I was conscious of it, but there was nothing I could do to stop it. When the doctors told me I had to forget about the life I once had, to forget about how I planned to live my life going forward...well, this is probably no surprise, but I didn't jump up and down with joy at that conclusion!

I fell, *in a bad way*—not just emotionally and psychologically. I literally fell physically onto the hardwood floor of my living room in Barcelona. I screamed and begged the Universe to just take me away, then and there—if the only outcome I was left with was to give up on what I had dreamed of for so long.

Eventually, I fell asleep and, strangely enough, when I woke a bit later, I actually felt better—or at least it seemed like it. Fast-forward to the next morning and I knew something had occurred the day before; I knew I was healing. Somehow or other, it was happening inside of me. Eventually, I even went back to walking normally. In a few months, I was working out daily at the gym, hiking, and loving life. Am I still sick? Probably, but, hey, who cares? As long as I continue to refuse to give into a condition I didn't ask for, then job done—right?

I had instigated a drastic change in my life that impacted everything and everybody in it. My husband, my kids, my cat, and my business! I went from this shuffling, prematurely aging lady to a vibrant mom of four in tip-top shape. My business skyrocketed and we achieved an increase of more than three hundred percent in about three months. And that is the mission of *this book*. I knew I was not the only one who had been able to create these kinds of changes. I knew what I had been capable of manifesting, others had also managed to do. So I decided to gather some of them together to share their own experiences—as a way to fill your heart with hope, inspire your soul, and motivate your mind to embrace the idea that you can do the same manifesting…on your own terms.

I strongly believe we all have a very heavy responsibility when we enter this world in our human form. We are responsible for manifesting whatever we want. Nothing comes gift-wrapped, free, or by sheer chance. Things come to us because somewhere, somehow, we asked for them—the good as much as the bad. The only thing is, not everybody's aware of this fact. How do I know? Because for many years I was asleep—I had no idea the nightmare I was creating for myself.

With research, study, and an intense curiosity, I started learning…and my vision changed. But despite a new intellectual understanding of the elements around me, I didn't attempt to implement anything… but I must've been doing that for all these years!

Some part of me must have known the truth all along, otherwise why would I have attracted that disease to my doorstep? I think that we fall as hard as we are—and I was sound asleep for years. In retrospect— and after all my research on the subject—I am convinced that MS is mostly a "thought disease."

I mean no offense to anyone that may suffer from MS. I'm not saying this from a medical perspective. I am not a doctor. I'm just sharing my deepest, most raw feelings about it. If it is not a thought disease, then how do you explain my being able to recover so fast? How do you explain all the miracle healings happening in this world? I read an anthropology article a few weeks ago that explained that cancer was completely absent from tribes in Amazonia and other parts of the world, and they defined it as a manmade disease. Some healers go as far as saying cancer is a way of releasing anger from our system; hence, the reason they also refer to it as the "anger disease."

When I fell hard on the floor that day, I actually waved the white flag in surrender, and I gave in to a higher part of myself. I gave up controlling everything and agreed with what was (even though I had no knowledge of it at the time). I agreed to the point where I saw how futile it was to keep fighting. And because I renounced that intellectual control, I ended up gaining another kind of control. Actually, it's not exactly about gaining a new control, more about regaining power over one's destiny—a power that had been there all along. From that moment on, I knew I could manifest anything I wanted in my life. But even though I was convinced of that, I still had no clue how to reproduce it. I had no clue how to replicate a process I had implemented without even realizing it.

Since then, I have been able to clearly pinpoint the steps I had initially taken in order to reach the expected result. I did reproduce it, my clients did, and more importantly, my husband did as well. This is what you will read about in my chapter.

In reality, there is a lot of literature going back over the last century that covers, at great lengths, what will be shared in a vibrant and colorful way in the following pages. The notion of a person being worthy of creating his/her own desire is also documented in the Bible. So what happened? How come most of the world has no clue about it and those who do know might not believe it? Somewhere in the midst of time, this ability freaked out a few people, to the point where their mission in life was to eradicate all recollection of that knowledge. Remember, knowledge is power. But then it came back—a change in consciousness did happen and it started many years ago. Now the principles of creating your own "luck" have been adopted by more and more people, and in turn, they have documented their results as well. It is these same principles that are still used today to create exactly the same outcomes.

The beauty of it is that you don't need any special or privileged education. You don't need to be born into a wealthy environment. You don't need fancy machines or magic spells to achieve what you may believe impossible today. What you actually need is always with you and can be called upon at any time—on command. All you really need is your mind, your heart, and your body. It's that simple. And that simplicity is what feeds the skeptics! In our modern-day society, we have come to believe that for something to be good it has to be complicated, therefore, by association, anything simple has to convey poor value. We have been raised and fed upon that limiting belief, which makes it so easy for the majority of us to dismiss the very basics of our human nature. However, you are also born with free will…and that ability also serves a purpose. You can use it to defy or reject whatever has been shared with you and decide for yourself to be your own boss — to try out, test, and verify the validity of any new and challenging concepts.

Every co-author in this book, myself included, will share with you their own experience with this amazing power. We will explain to you what we did and how we did it. Of course, it doesn't mean you can adopt a cookie cutter approach and just blindly follow in our footsteps to obtain exactly the same result. You may, of course, but that will not come with a guarantee. So why bother, you may ask? Because we all need to start somewhere. In the following pages, you will find golden nuggets of wisdom that you may want to replicate to the letter, and I encourage you to do so. If it works, then great. If it doesn't produce exactly what you were hoping for, I suggest you go back over the process you used and identify what feels right and what doesn't. Then change what does not and replace it with other elements that are better aligned with and take account of your own persona, your likes, and dislikes.

For example, I get up every day at 4:30 a.m. and work out for two hours. That doesn't mean you have to get up at 4:30 a.m. and work out for two hours. Maybe in your own particular case, getting up at 7:00 a.m. and going for a thirty-minute walk every day would be the perfect balance for you. Do you see what I mean? Apply the principles shared in this book, by all means, but be open to flexibility so you are able to fine-tune your own process.

One word of caution: The Universe *does* deliver each time. It doesn't make a distinction between positive and negative, between good and bad, for the simple reason that these notions are man-made and the Universe is unable to recognize them.

Manifest, you will! What you actually manifest is what really matters and that, my friend, is entirely up to you.

Happy manifesting!

THANK YOU

Since my last book, *Hot Mama in (High) Heels,* appeared on the scene, I have been toying with the idea of writing a solo book based around the power of gratitude. However, I manifested this book first. This book is a tribute to the Universe for having helped me throughout my life and for making sure that its last message was delivered to me loud and clear. Without that powerful knock and wake-up call, I probably wouldn't be here today to tell the tale.

The idea for this book came directly through that special connection I nurture every day with my special friend and best business partner — the mighty Universe.

As I write these lines, a deep-rooted feeling of gratitude is welling up in my heart. I feel so blessed for having reconnected with the Universe. I say "reconnected" because that connection is there, no matter what. It really doesn't matter if you sense it or not. It's a gift you received at birth. We are all born with it...and then we forget about it. I hope this book will help you remember.

So much has happened since I initiated this new book...so many events have occurred in my life just to prove to me that all this is true, not just a fantasy of my mind. I have met so many people on the path to manifesting.

Putting this book together has been no easy task. Finding co-authors willing to share their amazing story was not the hard part...finding true manifesting stories was the challenge. So let me first thank every single author in this book — they dared to step forward. They are living their lives on the basis of what they share in the following pages. If you have read my other books, you already know I'm all about walking my talk, and I have the same level of expectation from any of the co-authors I work with. I can tell you this book is full of wisdom, love, tips, and gratitude toward the Universe, God, Allah...the actual name is less important than the meaning behind it. We all bow in front of the face of this powerful life force, which resides inside our heart and soul.

I would like to thank my team for having my back at any time and for being exceptional professionals. Some of them even wrote a story for this book. Why? Because they have a wonderful manifesting story… no wonder we work together! I love you guys.

Thank you to Jane Bell, my wonderful executive assistant. She knows I wouldn't be able to do anything without her. She is a dear friend and is now part of the family. Often times, she is also my coach.

A special thank you to my operations manager, Celeste Johnson, who is also part of this book. Celeste has a direct line to the Universe and she uses it every day to ensure Coaching & Success is thriving. Celeste is an amazing woman, a dear friend, and somebody the whole C&S team relies on. I'm so thrilled she accepted to share her story.

Thank you to my graphic designer, Alvaro Beleza, who created this fantastic cover and made all the adjustments I asked for… so much patience!

Thank you to my team of editors, Kemari Howell and Ann Holmes, who made sure this book was a pleasant read for you. Thank you for helping us to improve our processes and to keep on delivering a high quality service.

Thank you to Bernie, who lives with us now in Mexico. She is the real mom in the household and thanks to her, I have the time to fully work and concentrate on all my writing. She is a blessing sent from the Universe, that's for sure.

Thank you to my friend, Kim Boudreau Smith, who is always ready, willing, and able when I call her—ready for a talk, ready for a hike, and ready for glass of wine! Cheers, Kim!

Last but not least, thank you to my family…each and every one of them are teaching me something new every day, and they gave me the perfect playground to manifest new things every day.

NICOLE VAN HATTEM, HHC, AADP

Nicole van Hattem is a workplace wellness warrior, coach, and highly sought after inspirational speaker.

Nicole transformed her own body and mind by applying simple principles and small changes that resulted in her dropping three dress sizes, 17 kg (38 pounds) of toxic fat, overcoming a long list of ill-health complaints, and gaining energy, joy, and success—all without dieting.

With over twenty-five years in the corporate world, as a board certified holistic health coach, corporate wellness consultant, and raw foods and detox specialist, Nicole's coaching, corporate events, retreats, and programs have helped thousands of people to detox their lives and achieve vibrant success.

- www.NicolevanHattem.com
- www.linked.com/nicolevanhattem
- www.facebook.com/nicole.vanhattem.5
- www.instagram.com/Nicole_van_Hattem
- www.twitter.com/NicolevanHattem

MANIFESTATION 1

$\mathcal{H}$OW I MANIFESTED A CAR FULL OF MONEY AND SAVED MY LIFE

By Nicole van Hattem

It was September 2008. I was fast approaching forty—painfully overweight, miserable, stressed out of my mind, and destroying the joy in my second marriage. I had just escaped my corporate life to spend ten days on a raw detox retreat in Thailand with my soul sister, Sue. Like many other retreat attendees, I had come to clear my mind of mental fog, my belly of toxic waste, and find some peace and inner calm. I gained all of this and much, much more.

At the detox retreat, I learned how to meditate, to enjoy eating clean simple foods, to remove the waste from my mind and body, to move in new ways. This time-out created an opportunity for quiet mental space in which my inner voice could finally be heard. With time to breathe and think clearly, I slowly began to realize just how dangerously close I had been to self-destruction. It was then I got the courage to ask the universe to give me clarity on my life's purpose and guide me to redefine success for myself.

This was a giant leap away from how I lived my normal life. My role as head of human resources with an international bank consisted of working long hours, late nights, and most weekends. I was passionate about my work, loved supporting and leading my colleagues, and drew inspiration on a daily basis from my mentor and close friend, who was

16

also the CEO. By most people's definitions, I was a "success" —but it came at a very high price. I fueled myself on endless cups of coffee, sugary snacks, restaurant and packaged foods, and the adrenaline that comes from achieving corporate goals and big financial rewards. There was definitely no time for work-life balance, or connecting with any powers greater than the corporate machine.

When I left the retreat after three weeks, I was filled with new awareness and a body that was vibrant with life-force energy. Determined and ready to take my hectic corporate life in a new direction, I returned to the "real" world, completely unprepared for what happened next. My dear friend and CEO of the company died suddenly of a heart attack. Dressed in his just-another-day-at-the-office suit, drinking his morning coffee, his life ended at the age of forty-nine. Our fast-paced "successful" lifestyles had been the death of him.

I responded to the shock of my friend's death by quitting my job. I ran away as fast as I could from the corporate world. I wasn't waiting around for another wake-up call. I put my master's degree on hold and instead began to study cleansing and detoxing, raw foods, holistic health, neuro linguistic programming (NLP), and coaching.

I was so excited by what I was learning about how to transform lives that I wanted to share it with the whole world immediately. I dove headfirst into creating a multi-faceted health and wellness business, and within a short time, I had grown the company exponentially—I had a six-figure income and a dozen employees. One day, blinded by a stress-related headache, I realized I hadn't actually redefined success for myself. All I'd really done was recreate my crazy corporate life under the guise of a wellness title. So I stopped, took a breath, checked my ego, and then I closed the company.

Wiser for the experience, I decided to go on another retreat. I took the time to listen within and define my successful life with wisdom, clarity, and purpose, as well as implement some basic yet powerful daily routines. From that moment on, doors opened effortlessly to me, and my new business took off. This time I had set myself up for healthy, *holistic* success.

The foundation of my personal success strategy are my daily rituals. These daily practices help to keep me in balance and in the flow of energy so I can continue to move on my path. They give me time to breathe, to listen to my inner guide, to take care of my physical body, and to make sure I'm on the right path. Some of these rituals are non-negotiable, and on others I'm a little more flexible, depending on what's happening in my life at the time.

Here are my daily practices:

POWER-START THE DAY

Bowel massage (to clean out the *junk in the trunk*) and gratitude practice (because life is awesome and I will celebrate it every day). I do these two practices together to maximize my time.

Lemon water, aloe vera gel drink, green smoothie, or green juice (to keep my insides clean, hydrated, alkalized, and fueled).

Sun salutations, meditation, and manifesting (energizing, awakening, centering, and in the flow).

If for any reason I don't get number three done in the morning before the day begins, I add it into the day wherever it will work.

TAP INTO POWER

The meditation and manifesting exercises I do in the early mornings are essential to putting my energies in the right place to power my day. It took me several months to embed this into my life as a routine, but I kept the rituals simple and was consistent with them, and it's been worth the effort. I also use this practice as often as I need to throughout the day. When I get caught up in the busyness or frustrations of day-to-day life, when I think I've done all that I can to move forward but still feel stuck and don't know what to do next, I:

- Stop

- Breathe

- Let go

- Listen

- Ask

- Wait

- Watch

Doing this has yielded more than a few rewards. One day, when I'd thought all sources had dried up, this practice rained money down on me. I was running my business and I had staff salaries to pay, but the cash wasn't flowing in on time and I was breathless with anxiety over how it was all going to work out for that month. Between appointments, I realized my mind was full of fear and my bank account was empty. I questioned what practical actions I could take to reverse that. As I was driving, I mentally went through the list of logical answers—follow up on outstanding debtors to pay their bills, borrow some money, sell some resources, run a few quick events, etc. I decided to pull over on the side of the road and breathe.

I sat in my car and switched off the engine. I closed my eyes, took three long deep breaths, and relaxed my belly as best I could. I put my hands on my thighs, palms up, and I imagined that money was falling from the sky into my hands. As I played with this image in my mind, I actually felt the touch of the notes land on my skin and the piling of the money around my legs in the car. The more I got into this image, the more I felt the fear and tension flow away and joy fill the space instead. After a few minutes, I opened my eyes and switched on the car ignition. At that moment, my phone rang—it was a corporate client calling to confirm an appointment with me for a workplace wellness series. Hooray! I could relax even more and get on with my day because money was on its way.

You can dismiss this as mere coincidence, but that belief would only disempower you. I know from my own experiences, and the inspiring stories from hundreds of other people, that there is power in believing you can influence and create your own reality. You have a choice. Which do you choose?

Manifesting success is hard work but it isn't always about doing. Sometimes it's about remembering that you are made of stardust—as astronomer Carl Sagan said—a part of all the energy and matter that has ever existed or will ever exist. You are not separate, you are a *part of*. And as a part of the universal life force, you have access to its power. In fact, *you are power*. Call it meditation, prayer, magic, energy work, science, or whatever resonates with you, but include stepping into this power as part of your daily rituals and practices and notice how you are propelled forward.

Create rituals that nurture your spirit, your mind, and your body, and that enable you to tap into unlimited power to manifest your visions and life's purpose. Keep your rituals simple. Practice them daily.

Remember that your life is a precious gift, there is a purpose for you being alive, and you are powerful. Your daily rituals will keep you on track with your life's purpose, in the flow of manifesting true success, and may even save your life.

CATIE KIRKE

Catie Kirke wants you to have it all. The award-winning business woman from Darwin, Australia, harnessed over two decades of fitness training and life coaching expertise and catapulted her ambition to national and international acclaim.

The abundantly empowering founder of ART Your Life has created world-class holistic programs for personal and professional growth, handcrafted to unleash profound and permanent change from the inside out. Catie's underlying motivation—"what walks in us runs in the next generation"—fuels her determination to elevate people to love who they are and help them *Activate, Reshape,* and *Transform* their lives.

⌂ www.artyourlife.com.au

MANIFESTATION 2

Mindfully Manipulate Yourself to Manifest the Life You Love

By Catie Kirke

Do you ever go to bed wishing you could clone yourself to get more done? Do you want to fit more in your day and take better care of yourself with regular exercise, nutritious home cooked meals, meditation, relaxation and quality time with family, friends and yourself? You are not alone!

Life in the twenty-first century is lived in the fast lane. It's full of pressures, stress, striving for the next best thing, expectations, attempting to achieve perfection, mixed messages, sensationalized and confrontational media, and demanding technology—all of which can consume us.

We women are so talented at multi-tasking and prioritizing others before us that we often do so to our own detriment. We get through each day on a half-empty energy tank and an overfull head, and we go to bed exhausted. Our to-do list gets longer, which results in feeling guilty, overwhelmed, and disorganized—and that has a negative impact on the quality of our lives.

When people ask me how I manage to do and achieve so much personally and professionally in any given day, my answer is always the same—I mindfully manipulate myself. It is an empowering ritual I use to observe and lead myself, and it has helped me turn my life around. I have gone from numbly existing to passionately living, and from being my own worst enemy to becoming my own best friend.

I mindfully manipulate myself strategically and sometimes quite unscrupulously. As harsh as this may sound, I call it "tough love." It always comes from a place sourced from kindness and keen self-awareness. This ritual is the key to how I have built one of Australia's most successful and highly regarded personal coaching businesses, and how I am manifesting a life I love.

FROM DEAD END JOB TO BUSINESS SUCCESS

For six years, I was responsible for the physical fitness and defensive tactics preparation training for police recruits in my state. The job was going nowhere and there were no pathways for promotion or development. I was bored, underutilized, and going brain dead. Physically, I was worn out and literally battered and bruised. Two of my ribs were broken after being thrown in a takedown demonstration, and I was worried about what the job was doing to my body.

On top of that, my very average paycheck was only just making ends meet week to week. There was no foreseeable way I could help fund my daughter through university, let alone invest in wealth creation. I was over forty and fearful of my future! It was time for drastic change and that meant believing, thinking, and "doing life" radically differently.

Thus, my ritual of mindfully manipulating myself was born. It has been evolving and serving me ever since. Within a twelve-month period, it enabled me to juggle my full-time police job, instruct fitness classes at a gym, earn a diploma, provide life coaching sessions for a growing clientele base, create the seven-week ART Your Life intensive, manage a home, and be a solo mum with a beautiful daughter in her final year of school.

To achieve all of this, my mindful manipulation was to swallow my "magic pill" daily. And the ingredients that make this magic pill so magical are: perspective, perseverance, priorities, and perspiration.

Perspective:

Your perspective creates your reality. If your perspective is based on the view that you do not have enough time, money, energy, resources, skills, contacts, or confidence then, quite simply, that will be true for you. And you will continue to get what you have always received.

To ensure this doesn't happen, self-awareness is crucial. Socrates commanded "Know thyself." I observe and monitor my perspective daily to ensure it is not being marred by negativity, self-indulgence, limiting beliefs, and fears. I am conscious of not comparing who I am or what I look like, and what I do or don't have, to others.

My mirror is my canvas. Every morning, to start my day with a perspective of abundance and self-belief, I write messages to myself on my mirror with whiteboard markers. My favorites are:

I am enough

I am important

I am cared for

I have nothing to prove and nothing to defend

Perseverance:

Our ability to persist and remain constant in our purpose, tasks, commitments, and, most importantly, to self is "easy" when things are going well. However, when obstacles, problems, and distractions happen it can all seem too hard…we give up on making our dreams come true.

The bottom line is that sh*t happens every day. It's a part of living life. Once we accept this, we can deliberately make molehills out of mountains—instead of making mountains out of molehills!

When I am faced with problems and obstacles, I appreciate the opportunity to be "creative-solution focused." I ask myself these four empowering questions:

"What is good about this?"

"What am I learning?"

"How can I experience this differently?"

"What would love say to me right now?"

Priorities:

How we prioritize what we do and what we focus on daily creates our outcomes in life. Business, career, relationships, wealth, health, home, and socializing all need attention. It's not easy to get it *right*. The casualty of juggling all these balls and demands is usually ourselves—feeling guilty, running on empty, people-pleasing, and wishing for that clone!

You MUST give to YOU. Prioritize your time accordingly.

Ask yourself what you can do on a daily basis to nurture yourself and fill your energy tank so you can juggle AND catch the balls. Maybe it's taking time to meditate each morning or soaking in a bath. Maybe it's lavishly moisturizing your whole body or dancing to your favorite music. Perhaps it's reigniting an old hobby—like playing the guitar again, or enjoying the creation of art and craft.

For me, it's exercise. With regular exercise, I know I am more effective, focused, and balanced, and I am more comfortable in my own skin. It is a priority for me to schedule "appointments" in my diary with girlfriends to walk and/or weight train. No matter how busy my day is, I know myself well enough to be certain I won't let a girlfriend down. My mindful manipulation ensures that I am taking care of *me*. The wonderful bonus is that I am also nurturing my beautiful friendships.

Perspiration:

Our capacity to do what needs to be done without procrastination, delay, or elegant adult excuses is crucial to manifesting a life we love. However, we all know there are always things in the *too hard* basket we would rather avoid. Whether it's that pile of paperwork, the conversation that needs to be had, an overflowing inbox, an appointment that needs to be made, and/or cobwebs on the ceiling.

When we put these things off, they become burdensome in our mind and slow down everything we do. This clouds our ability to manage our time and fulfill our wants and responsibilities effectively and efficiently.

25

The key is to eat at least one "frog" in the early part of your day—the bigger the better! Once this is done, you become an unclouded and a focused "doer" and you quite literally get on with it. Yes, being a "doer" takes perspiration and you will definitely get a little sweaty eating that first slimy frog. But, it's worth getting it out of the way so it's no longer a distraction hanging over your head.

Yes, you guessed it…the "frogs" are those tasks or responsibilities you have been leaving in the *too hard* basket! Eat the biggest one first and the rest become easy.

I encourage you to embrace this magic pill filled with the essential ingredients of perspective, perseverance, priorities, and perspiration. You will feel focused and accomplished and create so much more balance in your life. You will also be learning how to love YOU more each day. Swallow the magic pill daily to *mindfully manipulate yourself to manifest the life you love.*

To learn even more about how you can love yourself, your body, and your life with simple and doable rituals, I encourage you to read my e-book, *10 ways to Love Yourself.* It's my gift to you, and it's full of powerful mindset and life strategies and tools to help you step into your personal power. Visit www.artyourlife.com.au/10-ways to download your copy.

EDA HARDY

Eda Hardy is an award-winning expert at removing emotional barriers, facilitating emotional healing, and increasing self-esteem. She is a mum to two gorgeous children, an NLP master practitioner, EFT (emotional freedom technique) practitioner, coach, author, mentor, trainer, hypnotherapist, past-life regression therapist, and Reiki master.

Visit http://www.masteryourfuture.co.uk/ for more information about emotional healing retreats, transformational healing days, emotional mastery programs, and various private transformational healing sessions with Eda. Here, you can also claim Eda's information-packed book, *5 Important Steps to Creating a Happy and Fulfilling Life*, which contains plenty of examples and tips that will help you overcome any emotional challenges.

- www.masteryourfuture.co.uk
- www.edahardy.com
- masteryourfuturenow@gmail.com
- www.facebook.com/MasterYourFuture
- www.facebook.com/MiracleMumsandKidsAcademy
- www.twitter.com/MasterFutureNow
- http://goo.gl/3JcAOk

27

MANIFESTATION 3

$\mathcal{T}$RANSFORM YOUR LIFE!

By Eda Hardy

My mission is to guide you on the path towards happiness and fulfillment and help you create a life beyond your wildest dreams.
– Eda Hardy

Do you suffer from anxiety and stress? Have you ever lost your confidence or felt like nobody understood you? Perhaps you've felt frustrated, insecure, and emotionally traumatized, as if you've lost your resilience. To make things worse, perhaps feelings of depression, worry, helplessness, and loneliness have arisen within you for no apparent reason.

If you've experienced these kinds of feelings, then you'll understand where I'm coming from. For more than a decade, I was in an extremely dark place that most people would find difficult to even comprehend. I have firsthand knowledge of how it feels to live with fear, pain, loneliness, and depression. It feels like there's a dark shadow following oneself, without knowing why one feels this way, or how to overcome these strong emotions.

It took me years to admit to myself that I needed help. I was always the strong one who inspired and led people, but my emotional struggle led me to become overweight, unhappy, and miserable. I lost my self-confidence and I felt invisible. I thought that my life no longer mattered, and I began to dread waking up each morning. I shut down my feelings completely, because I could no longer handle the emotional pain. By going into an emotionless mode, I forgot how to be happy, how to feel love, and how to be at peace. Eventually, I felt that I'd lost everything, including my marriage, my health, my self-confidence, my joy, and my passion for life. I put on a brave face, since I didn't want anyone to see me suffering, especially my children. However, I wasn't able to keep up the charade forever, and over time, began to show physical signs of emotional suffering.

It is our choices that show what we truly are, far more than our abilities.
– J.K. Rowling

Finally, one day, I decided I was going to transform my life and find the answers as to why I was suffering, so I could help others overcome similar problems. I've always had an incredible desire to learn, contribute, share, and grow. After my decision, I attended various workshops and studied with and received training from key leaders in the area of self-development. As I set off on this new path, I felt like instead of struggling, **I was being guided toward something amazing**. I studied and became an NLP (neuro-linguistic programming) master practitioner and hypnotherapist with Richard Bandler, the co-creator of NLP.

After I finished my NLP training, I decided to go see Anthony Robbins (the creator of the well-known self-help program, "Unleash the Power Within") in Rimini, Italy, and became a fire walker. I completed both the Anthony Robbins mastery university and his business mastery program, learning how to create lasting change within myself and others. I also completed my Reiki master and Reiki teacher programs, taught by the famous Carole Easton, who helped me turn my life around. Shortly afterwards, I completed my EFT training, during which I learned the fundamental tools and strategies that now enable me to help people overcome their emotional issues. I also read hundreds of self-help and psychology books. The more I learned about the mind-body connection, the more fascinated I became.

During my journey of growth, I met amazingly supportive people who enabled me to grow with them. It came to my attention that highly successful people have certain rituals in their lives that they follow religiously. I realized that ritual helps each of us awaken deeper levels of our own consciousness. Rituals also provide a sense of stability and continuity in our lives. Once I understood the importance of this subject, I started implementing highly recommended rituals in my life. I began paying more attention to my thoughts and words, and this helped me overcome my depression, my self-limiting beliefs, and my negative thought patterns. The more I practiced gratitude, the more impressed I became with its power. By paying attention to what we have, instead of what we are lacking, we experience a shift in consciousness. **When we have gratitude in our lives, this means we are accepting ourselves, loving ourselves, and honoring ourselves through every thought and action, which is extremely important to emotional well-being.** My profound rituals helped me overcome the pain of my past and leave it behind so I could move forward and start a new chapter in my life.

After experiencing a massive shift in my own consciousness, I realized that while emotions can sometimes be disturbing and unpleasant, humans are lucky to be born with such effective emotional guidance systems. One of the ways emotions guide us is by creating certain physical sensations that are difficult to ignore. **The negative emotions we experience are actually capable of creating energy blockages within our bodies that cause discomfort, pain, and illness.** Fortunately, I use and teach various techniques within my practice that remove most of these stagnant energies, so everyone I treat can lead happy, healthy lives.

One's life becomes a perfect mirror of one's beliefs, thoughts, words, actions, habits, and values. – Eda Hardy

As I continued to study the power of thoughts and emotions, I began to understand that everyone is capable of healing themselves. Therefore, to be able to rid yourself of emotional pain and master your future, you must learn to control your thoughts and words (which are representative of your beliefs and values and lead to certain actions and habits). If you repeat the same thought process, day after day, your subconscious mind will eventually accept it as representative of reality and prompt you to act in accordance with it.

Had I known in my earlier years what I know now, my life would have been much different. However, I have no regrets, as I've realized everything that has happened (or will happen) in my life is for a reason. All my life experiences have allowed me to undergo significant emotional growth, and without each one, I wouldn't be who I am today, helping people get over their emotional struggles. I am even grateful to those who have hurt me, knowingly or unknowingly; because of them, I'm stronger than I've ever been.

I've come to understand that all my life experiences put together are like a jigsaw puzzle—each piece, or experience, helps to create the big picture. Some of the pieces might seem unpleasant when I view them in isolation. However, once more pieces are laid out, and I can see the full picture more clearly, I begin to understand why each piece has been given to me. If we let ourselves go with the flow in life, we may realize what we once thought were our worst experiences have turned out to be tremendous gifts toward our personal growth; we may even determine that these experiences were essential pieces that had been missing from our puzzles.

I'm still putting my puzzle together piece by piece, and I'm helping others build theirs as well. Through the law of attraction, amazing people like you who just need a bit of assistance, healing, and recovery enter my life every day. **There are no coincidences.** You didn't start reading this book by chance. The truth is you're being guided towards the idea, even if you're not aware of it yet—this is your time to realize your full potential. In order to do so, you must trust yourself, surrender to the forces of life, and let go of past hurts that may be holding you back.

You don't have to go through the same kind of dark, painful, and lonely journey that I did. I now lead people down a less painful path toward self-empowerment and self-confidence. I also help people shift their consciousness. I do this through the amazing life transformation programs I've created, which are tailored to each participant's individual needs. One of my favorite structured signature programs is called "Emotional Transformational Retreat Day." This day helps renew your sense of inner peace, and it allows you time to relax your body and mind and recover the natural rhythm of your life.

If you want to begin to transform your life, you have to make the decision to live fully and start implementing the right rituals within it. You can start by simply paying attention to your dominant thoughts and words and/or practicing gratitude on a daily basis. By doing so, you will transform your life, which is the first step on your journey toward becoming who you've always wanted to be. **You deserve this, because you are a star, and the world needs your unique shade of brilliance. Don't wait—it's your time to shine—start now!**

With love, gratitude, and blessings,

Eda Hardy

KIM BOUDREAU SMITH

Kim Boudreau Smith is the proprietor for Bold Radio Station, a turn-key radio show host service for women business owners. She's also a #1 international best-selling author, international speaker, international business consultant, and strategist.

Kim provides a turn-key experience for business owners who want to market themselves as the expert that they are through their voice. Kim also teaches women how to sell like a woman.

Helping over one thousand people successfully achieve healthier lifestyles with her first business, she is taking this extensive business knowledge and paying it forward; helping women entrepreneurs defy obstacles, stop settling for less, step into their boldness, and enjoy success.

MANIFESTATION 4

Manifesting Through My Voice!

By Kim Boudreau Smith

"You should do a radio show! Come on, Kim, you love to talk, it's your thing!" My reply was a lot of "no way," but this didn't sit well with either of us. So with my grit and attitude, I stopped the "no ways" and did it. I launched my radio show with one condition—that she, Christine Marmoy, would agree to be my first radio show guest. And she agreed. With her immense support, I went global on my first show. "Oh my gosh!" she said after that first show, "You're a natural at this."

After that, I began growing a global marketing platform for my business, as well as providing a marketing platform for others. It seemed like everything was coming together, but things still felt a bit unclear. A conversation with Christine helped me gain clarity.

I kept asking: how do I take my business global and really make it stronger? I knew I needed help. I needed to find my true passion and align myself with my goals and passion for achieving them. I was building a business, but I was offering something I didn't completely believe in. I felt like I was forcing myself into it. The business became slow and I was losing energy. This weighed on my mind, my confidence, and my self-esteem. I started playing the comparison game—comparing myself to others. My inner critic was controlling and dominating me.

So Christine and I embarked on a working relationship together, and she listened carefully to my words, my wants, my desires, and my beliefs! The goal was to create an ideal marketing plan for my business. Soon, it became apparent that I was asking for one thing and doing another. I call this "messing with the Universe." I was manifesting exactly how I was feeling—very unclear. I was also manifesting and asking but not accepting...and this is so wrong. I would manifest and the universe would deliver and then I wouldn't accept. This is why it felt like work—it was long, hard, and laborious instead of passionate, joyful, and energetic. I was out of alignment and probably heading towards burnout, and I was losing hope.

Christine was the delivery from the Universe. A couple of years ago, I'd gotten a taste of collaboration by participating in an anthology like this one. The group—an amazing tribe of women—was engaging. I experienced what collaboration really meant and I'd loved it. I spoke to Christine about collaboration and how passionate I was about it. Providing a platform for others and being able to support others was awesome and it made me feel good. We worked hard together on the radio platform, and it took a lot of work.

Doing the radio show was more than just adding to an already-busy plate—it was a whole other plate that a busy business owner had a difficult time managing. I hired an assistant to help with the tasks of my show, but it was still a lot to manage and a lot to learn—the technology, managing guests, and so on. There were a lot of facets to the radio show that needed to be worked out, and to do it alone took quite some time. A dream of mine became unveiled—owning my own radio station. After I launched my radio show, I began to wonder how anyone does it alone. Building numbers, visibility, scheduling guests... it took a lot of time and work!

Manifesting is quite easy. It's surrendering to the gift I find difficult. And I see others who have the same difficulty. We ask of the Universe and we must show the Universe we are preparing for the gifts it will deliver. But how do we prepare? One way for me personally is meditation, physical exercise, and introspection. I love to talk and hear words. This helps me become stronger with my intuition and my inner wisdom. I become clearer on my wants and desires. The moment I find myself wondering, "How am I going to do this?" I turn it back over to the Universe. When we go into the asking of how, we are allowing our ego to take over. For me, this is when I *force things* instead of *allowing them to happen*. It's a lot like the women in Cinderella's village, trying to cram their feet into the glass slipper. Ouch! It doesn't fit and it doesn't work. This is the home of the ego. The ego wants you to believe if you want results, you have to control your life. Make it happen! Force and increase the stress! Do, do, do!

Don't get me wrong, I don't go and just sit on the couch after I ask for assistance. I continue to do my due diligence and move forward. For example, I ask the Universe for my ideal client. But more than just asking for it, I do my due diligence and move forward. I take the time to visualize everything I want in an ideal client and I do a characteristic profile of everything I want in an ideal client. The Universe gives me that and much more. This is what I mean—doing your due diligence and moving forward. We have to show we are ready for the gifts! For my radio station, I spoke this and the Universe delivered something way bigger than I. If anyone would have said to me, "Kim, you will own a radio station one day," I would have laughed and said, "You are out of your mind!" Seriously! To me, that is life. It is way bigger than us and we are not here to figure it all out. I am definitely not here to figure it all out! The Universe has a grand plan for me…and for all of us!

I was constantly told growing up that I should be seen and not heard, which doesn't surprise me considering how much I love to talk. I would rather talk through things in life than write, quite frankly! For me personally, talking soothes the soul. The sound of someone's voice is so amazing. The vibration in sound is very moving and it really says a lot about a person and their emotions.

In the past two years, I've learned that what we speak and ask for is what we are manifesting. We are asking the Universe to deliver our creation, our lives. The cliché may be *to be careful what you ask for*, but I don't believe you need to be *careful*. I believe you need to be *crystal clear* on what you want because the Universe delivers right to your front door. And there is another large piece to this; we have to be strong within ourselves to accept the opportunities when they arise. Not just to be ready for the opportunities *to happen* but to be clear to say *yes to them*!

Richard Branson says: "If somebody offers you an amazing opportunity but you are not sure you can do it, say yes—then learn how to do it later!" You have asked for your creation, manifested, and this is the universe delivering to you. When this happens, we don't need to have all the answers, we just need to have faith that the process will unfold as we need it to.

Our passion is worn on our sleeve, always. It doesn't appear on goods or go away when we are having a challenging day. Passion is a part of us. Now go and manifest your dream!

LISA FITZPATRICK

Lisa Fitzpatrick revels in supporting women to find their unique life purpose and heal their businesses so they can enjoy sustainable, meaningful, and fulfilling success. She is the author of *Healing the Heart of Your Business* and the founder of Sacred Women's Business, providing coaching for intelligent and conscious women entrepreneurs with a legacy to leave. Lisa is a certified coach, writer, yoga teacher, workshop facilitator, entrepreneur, speaker, registered physiotherapist, and mother. She lives in a subtropical paradise near Byron Bay, Australia, with her two sons.

🏠 www.LisaFitzpatrick.com.au

✉ sacredwomensbusiness@yahoo.com.au

f www.facebook.com/thenewfeminineleader

🐦 www.twitter.com/seraphicdream

🅿 www.pinterest.com/seraphicdreamin/

MANIFESTATION 5

THE ONE ESSENTIAL SECRET TO SACRED BUSINESS SUCCESS

By Lisa Fitzpatrick

There was a time when I barely stood still long enough to listen to what my heart was saying. Life was a game of piñata. I was blindfolded, desperately trying to hit something hard enough to find the sweets. Everything felt beyond my control. My attention deficit disorder moved from one shiny idea to the next, unclear which one to follow. Each thought competed with another.

There's a myriad of ways to master the art of drowning out the crowded marketplace of the mind. Relationship dramas, nagging the kids, mindless household chores, working too much, surfing the internet, and shopping—take your pick, I took them all on. Engaging in the soap opera of other people's lives ensured that I never stopped long enough to hear what was beyond the white noise in my own life. So long as the valleys beyond the fracas were echoing with my to-do list, I was OK.

It was essential for me to stay busy, because behind the busyness lay an unfamiliar landscape of quiet. The silence beneath the noise filled me with fear. I chose to stay busy to avoid those sinister undercurrents at any cost. They felt empty. I justified being busy and never considered what might happen if I stopped. The void beyond the noise felt like it might swallow me whole. I didn't know who I would be without my never-ceasing to-do list.

An implosion is a violent, inward-facing collapse. For every person, this manifests differently. For me, it came in the form of a breakdown. My major intimate relationship with my beloved came to an end. It forced me to stop. In the face of my breakdown, my to-do list was suddenly meaningless. The void had finally caught up with me. That which I most feared came to pass — *I was forced to be still.* I was disabled by a broken heart. The implosion paralyzed me just long enough for me to finally meet with peace and quiet. I was engulfed by silence. It marked the end of my old life.

This accidental awakening to the power of silence has been the pivot point that put me back in control of my life. Peace and quiet allowed the blindfold to fall. I began to see how I could consciously redirect my life with a daily ritual of silence. My ability to manifest more of what I want has been amplified. I believe my ritual is my one essential secret to sacred success.

A fortune teller once told me that many lifetimes ago, I was a white witch and healer who gathered herbs in the wilds of Cornwall. Perhaps this explains why I am fascinated by magic and the power of ritual. I have always loved how magic can weave its way into everyday life to create small miracles and blessings, but I had always been too busy to stop long enough to soak up its revelations. Being thrust into silence through my personal crisis was by far the most potent ritual I have experienced. Since my pivot upon silence, I now enjoy other rituals too — gathering and arranging fresh flowers for the altar, doing my yoga practice, and saying prayers to invoke the divine. There's a number of ways I have welcomed the sacred into my life.

The setup for my ritual is simple. The kettle is boiled, some tea is poured, and the phones are turned off. Uncurling my yoga mat comes next. I place some cushions and a bolster on the mat. Cross-legged or astride the bolster is how I usually enjoy sitting. Dipping into silence, the mind often takes a while to slow down. I notice the breath snake in through the nostrils — cool on the inhale, and warm on the exhale. I watch my thoughts — a pack of wolves, skulking, circling, and pacing. They insinuate I shouldn't aim so high. *You'll never make it*, they say. *What were you thinking?* I observe them with intense curiosity. So long I have been running from them, afraid and uneasy. But when I sit with them, I see them clearly. There's something more powerful at work in me than these wild animals of my own mind, if only I'll take the time to tune in and listen.

This powerful thing at work in me is exquisite. It possesses rare and precious beauty. Its vulnerability belies a power greater than anything wild animals could bring. It requires supreme stillness to reveal itself. It has been hiding in the spaces in between my busyness and chaos for so long. I lament how many times I avoided it, yet it has always been there. Behind everything else: the chaos, the dark nights of the soul, the blind fumbling through life, the striking out at the piñata. It lights the darkness. It requires tenderness and introspection. It is truth, it is light, and it is love. The small, still voice within me has only ever desired for me to dip into stillness so that it can finally be heard.

I sit for around ten minutes some days and up to thirty minutes on others. The irony is the busier I am, the more important this time of dipping into stillness becomes. My ritual has supported me to find my compass. The compass points me in the direction of my dreams. It never fails me. If I were to tell you where it is in my body, I would say it sits inside my belly and points to my heart. Every day, I successfully navigate the wilderness using my compass. My trust in this internal directive is unfailing. It allows me to confidently hold space for my coaching clients—spiritual women entrepreneurs who are navigating their own wild terrains. It allows me to support them so they can find, hear, and honor their inner compasses too. True north is the direction of benevolence, true wisdom, and higher purpose. This is where the compass points. It had been there all along, but I was blindfolded to it.

It's due to this ritual that I wake up every day feeling excited about what the day may offer at Sacred Women's Business. Coaching requires patience, focus, dedication, commitment, passion, love, trust, and grace. To build this business that makes my soul sing, I make space for stillness in order to listen to the voice of my heart. I have had to stare down the wild animal thoughts and tame them so they no longer run me off course. I can choose to run alongside them or away from them. Or I can choose to stop and listen.

So many times, I witness women trying to outrun the wolves rather than to simply sit with them, allowing them to be seen for what they are. They are merely thoughts. In the face of supreme stillness, where the loving presence of the divine can be heard and felt, they have absolutely no power—except the power that we give them.

There is a lot of wilderness to navigate in the heroine's journey. Sacred business success relies upon the ability to go beyond comfort zones and to transcend the unease of being in unknown territories. My soul yearns to take me on an exhilarating ride while I reach for my highest and wildest visions, my hair trailing behind me. However, if I don't take the time to find my compass, to listen to the voice of my own heart, I risk being misdirected, diverted, distracted, and even tricked into taking a less desirable path than the glorious one my compass points me to. I know where misdirection leads—to a life only half lived inside the illusion of distraction. It leads to a life of regret.

My ritual strengthens my connection to my inner wisdom. It has shown me how to create a business that embraces my true purpose and has drawn to me extraordinary clients, holistic wealth that warms my soul, and the feeling that I no longer need to run. I can finally rest. Then from that place of quiet comfort, I know with certainty I can launch myself into the wilderness to face the brave, toward new lands in the direction of my dreams. I confidently guide other women to do the same by teaching them to find their inner compass and discover the pathway to their own true calling.

Sacred Women's Business tip: Every day, take time out to immerse yourself in total and complete stillness. Ask yourself, "Can I hear the small, still voice of my heart? What is she saying?"

LISA PATTENDEN

Lisa Pattenden owns and operates My Absolute Image. She is a coach and mentor for survivors of breast cancer. Lisa has a family history with breast cancer and has experienced family members who have had reconstructive surgery, and lost other family members to this life-changing disease. In particular, she has lost her mum, grandmother and aunt to this devastating disease.

Lisa's talent lies in her ability to connect with women who have gone through traumatic events—cancer, plastic surgery, and reconstructive surgery. She is able to help you find yourself again and embrace your new life by creating a personalized plan using her five-step process that leaves you confident and in control of your new life.

Lisa can be reached through many channels of social media:

🏠 www.myabsoluteimage.com

🏠 www.lisapattenden.com

🏠 www.traumatransformer.com

🐦 www.twitter.com/London_lady

f www.facebook.com/MyAbsoluteImage

45

MANIFESTATION 6

How to Successfully Overcome Trauma in Your Life

By Lisa Pattenden

The truth about trauma is that you're never really 100 percent ready for it to happen. I know this may come as a shock to many that I, the trauma transformer, am saying this. But let's put it into perspective: it's not the trauma that gets you but how you react to it that determines your direction.

You see, I work with women who have been through breast cancer and they have made so many choices on "autopilot" that when they come to me, they are in a form of PTSD (post-traumatic stress disorder) that isn't easy to come away from. You're on fast-forward autopilot for such a long time, or what may seem a long time, and then it's like the fast train stopped suddenly but you're still moving. You've gotten off the train and are at the departure board, looking at all the destinations you could go to but you have no idea which one to pick — you're in overwhelm.

I work with women who are tired of being in overwhelm and want to know how to make the first move and how to figure out the next best journey for them. So many women are told by family and friends what they think she *should* do rather than figuring out what it is that they themselves *want* to do. I help my clients find the strategy for their next best journey. In this strategy, we transform them from the trauma and find that little bit of sparkle that really gets them feeling full of joy, alive, confident, and free again to go out there and achieve what they are looking to do next.

Coming up with my system wasn't always as defined as it is now. I really didn't know that I had a system until I helped my mother when she first was diagnosed with breast cancer. Her cry for help after her surgery was the first call to my soul to get my gift out there. Together, she and I busted down the myths that created her pain and enabled it to linger on for her. When she asked me how, not having been trained, I was able to do this work with her, I told her the story of when I was injured in Iraq and how that really came to bring me back into the spirit of carrying on after a trauma.

I'll tell you the story of that time so you can understand where I really got the message of how to transform trauma—a message that would play out the rest of my life anytime I was faced with trauma. You see, I was in the military, the US Air Force to be exact, as an aircraft mechanic. I ended up going overseas for quite a few conflicts while I was serving my time. One time, I was sent as a person on loan to the army to do convoy duty in Iraq. I had an incident that could have ended my life, and in a way it did, because I began *living* afterward rather than looking at how I was going to die.

We were on the usual journey after lunch, going up the "Highway of Death"—Highway 80 in Iraq—named for so many that had died there in 1991. It was pretty hot that day—over 107 F—and instead of eating lunch, I went to the gym and worked out. My lunch consisted of a Powerbar and two bottles of water. I got in my truck and we were headed up to Basra. The journey was always the same sandy color and bland surroundings. Vehicles would pass us, and we always listened for any codes called out that meant the vehicles might be a concern. About thirty minutes into this journey, I heard a code called on the radio directed to me. I didn't think I heard it correctly so I asked them to repeat. It was as I'd thought—a code to bail out of my truck on the opposite side I was sitting in. The portion of road we were on was raised, so when I jumped out of the passenger side, I rolled down the hill. I landed on my right ankle, breaking it and pulling every muscle in my leg below the knee. I think a combination of not eating and the heat made me pass out, because after I heard the first shot fired, I blacked out.

It turned out that a lorry that was headed for my truck had hit me. What that lorry driver didn't know was the people who paid him to do this had all been arrested the day before. The man who did this was a local who was paid a month's salary by an independent group to stop the convoy. Not an uncommon thing in this area.

I was airlifted to the hospital and taken care of medically. It was a sick joke being on crutches in the desert but I managed to work it out. After a few days, they had me come in to fill out the complete report of what had happened. The man driving the lorry was in custody and I saw who it was—a man I had met before and actually given him my trainers for his wife. They had three kids and barely anything. The army wanted me to press charges against him so they could ship him to one of their terrorist prisons in Iraq—. I declined. They were so angry with me, trying to convince me that I wouldn't be able to live with myself if he went on to kill other American soldiers. But I told them I wouldn't be able to live with myself if I put the only provider for that family in a jail for an indefinite period of time, miles away from his family, because he was only trying to feed them.

I went home to the states a month later and recounted this story to a doctor I saw. He had an interesting response. He asked me, "Why wouldn't you press charges? How can you live with the memory of this event knowing you let him go?'" It was at that point when I realized the true message I got loud and clear when I was still in Iraq. With this revelation, I responded, "Why are you insisting I bring this man back to the states with me for an indefinite period of time to fill my days and nights? Why can't YOU leave him with his family as I have?" The doctor definitely didn't understand what I meant. He just didn't get it.

You see, my message became about what we carry around with us. Events that are traumatic can happen to us, and we can choose to hold onto it or *let it go*. This was my first event, as an adult, to change my mindset—one of holding on and holding back to learning to let go instead. When I told my mother this story, she began to cry. She asked me to teach her how to have this same attitude because she was tired of carrying around the many things she picked up along the way in her journey with breast cancer.

Unfortunately, six years later, my mother got secondary cancer in her liver and bones and she was deemed terminal—with eight months to live. During this time, she asked me to make her a promise. She wanted me to do more work with women to show them how to get through the trauma because everyone can survive but who is teaching them how to thrive? Who is helping them set up the systems in their life to enable them to carry on in a positive and confident way? I promised my mother I would do this work—and I have been working with women for almost two years now, developing and fine-tuning the system I use to enable my clients to transform their trauma.

Thank you so very much for allowing me to share my story with you. I do hope that you will get in touch with me if you've been through a trauma and find you need my assistance. I'm known for transforming your trauma, and I aim to leave you feeling joyful, confident, and living your perfect life again!

ZAHRA EFAN

Zahra supports heart-centered women entrepreneurs to create success with ease by helping them connect inner principles of abundance with outer practical marketing strategies. Her promise is to help her tribe create a business without overwhelm, overwork, or burnout in their business. She is a published author, speaker, trainer, and a business coach with an extensive background in sales and marketing. She has done thirty-plus years of off- and on-line media interviews, including her interview speaking about gratitude on national TV. To watch her interview and download a free resource on creating abundance in your life and business, visit http://www.zahraefan.com

MANIFESTATION 7

꧋NITIATION TO ABUNDANCE

By Zahra Efan

I believe we get put onto the path of abundance—sometimes by tragedy, other times by desire and passion. It doesn't matter which path one takes, the path of being a seeker is a path of great challenge as well as a path of great promise.

I am going to share a mythological story about a girl with broken hands:

> *Long ago, a girl lived happily with her family in their home, and they had a beautiful apple tree in their garden. One day, the devil came to visit the family disguised as someone promising he could change the destiny of the family. The devil said to the father of the girl: "If you cut this apple tree, prosperity will bestow upon you." The father, not being in touch with his intuition, bought into the greedy promise made by the devil and cut the tree. Alas, along with the tree, the hands of his daughter got cut off. The mother comes running to the father, crying: "What have you done? That was the devil and your greed has made you cut the tree, along with the hands of our daughter!" The little girl cried tears so deep it shook the earth and the sky.*

> *After the betrayal by her father, she lost her trust and her belief in the institution of family. The family said to her, "We will look after you, protect you, feed you, and comfort you in your sorrows; we will be your hands." But she left the house and went to the wilderness to find her way. When she got hungry and wanted to reach for an apple to feed herself, she couldn't reach the tree because she had no hands. But the spirit world*

intervened, and the tree bent down so the girl could feed herself. When she was full, the tree went back to its original form.

A prince was watching the whole scenario; being a wise man of high intelligence and being in touch with the higher level of masculine energy, the prince knew the intuition and spirit of the girl would bring him greater prosperity and wisdom to run the kingdom. It would guide him to do the right thing for the good of all mankind under his leadership.

He fell in love with divinity of the girl, married her, and got her hands of gold—and they lived happily ever after.

This is the first part of the story of the girl with the broken hands. This story tells us about a girl who was betrayed by life. Her innocence and her belief that her family could provide protection had been shattered. This is how the initiation into abundance happens. One goes through a change and finds out things are not as one thought they would be. It starts with a breakdown or a tragedy. It seems like everything has fallen apart; however, the journey to the new world—the journey to the heart—has just begun.

When the girl still had hands and was living with her family, she wasn't in touch with her magic—her value. She was innocent and oblivious to the world of the underground—the deep wisdom within a woman's psyche. After having to find her way facing the danger of being alone in the wilderness, she learns to trust in a power greater than herself and she finds her faith—the support that is always available to women when we access our inner wisdom. Only after she is ready to attract her equal does the prince see her magic, fall in love with her, and marry her.

The journey to abundance is very much like that. We experience a huge lack and get thrown into discomfort. We decide to create our own magic, dancing to the beat of our own rhythms. We create our own destiny. At first, the loss can feel like a breaking down of everything, but I believe God is breaking us down so that he can build us back up. We are no longer going to be creating from our old belief system, whether it's our family, our culture, or the religious context we were raised in. Sisters, the journey is not always easy, but it is well worth traveling.

If you have been through tragedy or loss of any kind, I want you to think of it as a catalyst and initiation into your new life. The life you will get to create from inside out will now be based on who you are as a human being at your core, or I should say, a spiritual being having a human experience.

As spiritual beings, we are here to grow and change, but change comes with having gone through a loss—the loss of our old identity. It doesn't have to be a dramatic or huge loss. It could start with outgrowing a career you thought would bring you security, one you have invested time and energy to build. However, you feel a yearning and a desire to create a career that you love, that fulfills your soul desires. Letting go of something you have already invested time and energy in—hoping it would bring you prosperity and abundance, but doesn't fulfill your soul—is an initiation into your new world. Feeling discontentment where you are and a desire for something more—still not knowing what more looks like—could be an initiation to your new journey.

I have studied abundance and the principles of abundance. My initiation began when I was in a place in my life where none of my ego attachments were working. My career wasn't working, my money wasn't working, and my relationships were not working. I was in a long-distance relationship with my husband, I was making less money than I needed to survive, and I had no idea what my passion was—I just knew I wanted a career that would fulfill me and pay me well at the same time. When something like that happens, it is truly an initiation into the soul journey, because there is nothing my ego could attach to, to feel good. It almost felt like death—nothing I believed in would provide me the security I needed. Having recently migrated to Canada after living with my diplomat family in the UK, I had to learn life skills I knew nothing about—add to that I was thrown into a long-distance relationship and lacked clarity about my career path, and I really had to dig down deep to create the abundance I was seeking.

Fast-forward to today, I live in half-a-million dollar house (not a lot of money in the Canadian housing market)—but having paid most of the equity for the house, I do feel privileged. I have two beautiful children and a husband I wake up with every morning. I have a career I truly love—I help people internationally create their dreams and teach them principles of abundance, along with other practical marketing steps. I feel truly blessed. None of this would have been possible without the breakdown of my identity I experienced earlier in my life.

I hope you know, sister, that I am not telling you all of this to impress you. I am telling you this so you too can create your abundance from inside out. I'm telling you this so you can let tragedy become your greatest teacher in life—to help you create true wealth and happiness that comes from experiencing joy in every moment. I am telling you this so you realize you are better because of what you went through, and also to teach you what steps you need to take if it happens again, so you can climb back up to claim abundance and joy.

I want to share a couple of tips on inviting abundance in your life, and the things you can do to help you through this transition:

- Slow down—as simple as it may sound. When going through a crisis, you don't want to *keep running* to protect yourself from breaking down. Yes, if you need to pay bills and take care of the kids, please do that—however, make some time for yourself, to listen to your soul and feel your feelings. Feel all your feelings—good, sad, hurt, happy. All feelings will pass and will teach you something. Abundance is not feeling high or happy all the time. Abundance is an ability to feel all feelings, embracing them completely and being one with all life has to offer.

- Create the support of sisters you trust. Being able to be vulnerable and sharing what you are feeling with another human being—one who sees you for who you are—is the greatest gift you can give yourself during transition.

- Consistently connect with your higher power and surrender, pray, and ask for guidance.

PATRICIA LEBLANC

Patricia LeBlanc is a manifesting/life optimization coach and international best-selling author. Using a holistic approach, Patricia helps her clients get clear on what they want while remaining true to themselves. She teaches them how to manifest what they truly want and let go of their fears. Patricia is trained in several modalities such as law of attraction, law of attraction wealth, life coaching, life optimization coaching, Reiki, integrated energy therapy, theta healing, and EFT.

You can enroll in Patricia's free six-week online course, "How to manifest the life of your dreams" at www.patriciaeleblanc.com/ManifestingHighHeels

You can connect with Patricia on:

- www.facebook.com/leblancpatricia1
- www.linkedin.com/in/leblancpatricia
- plus.google.com/u/0/+PatriciaLeBlancLOA/about
- www.pinterest.com/leblancpatricia
- www.twitter.com/leblancpatricia

MANIFESTATION 8

How to Manifest the Life You Always Wanted

By Patricia LeBlanc

"You create your own universe as you go along."
— Winston Churchill

I did not always have the life I wanted. I went through a lot of struggles in my life, but when I started studying the law of attraction, and other modalities, and applying them to my life, it changed enormously. This was a turning point in my life and it allowed me to change my perspective. I started to manifest what I truly wanted. It also allowed me to stop being a victim and release all negative feeling I had towards certain life events—like being bullied in my childhood. I became responsible for what I was attracting in my own life.

I learned that you will always manifest what you are thinking and focusing on. If you think negative thoughts, then you will manifest negative events/things in your life. If you think positive things, then you will manifest positive events/things.

When you become conscious of what you want, you will manifest it and your life will change. You will notice a positive shift in your life and be happier. So why not choose positive thoughts and focus on the positive in your life? If you do this, you will manifest amazing things into your life.

Daily Habits I use to manifest the life that I truly want.

I have several daily habits I use every day to manifest the amazing life I have. I strongly recommend you do them daily. At first, it may not come easy, but trust me, with perseverance it will more than pay off. Commit to doing this every single day for at least twenty-one days—or even better, commit to doing this every single day for the rest of your amazing life. I know you can do it and you will be rewarded if you do. Remember, there is enough abundance for everyone and you can manifest anything you truly want.

Are you READY? Let's start!

MY MANIFESTING RITUALS

My future letter:

At the beginning of every year, I write my *future letter* and date it December 31, of that year. In this letter, I write everything I will manifest into my life for the upcoming year. I don't hold anything back. I address it to my Godmother, as she believes in me fully and encourages me to make my dreams come true. Choose someone who supports you fully and who will be very happy to hear of everything you accomplish during the year. Every month thereafter, I review it and add more stuff—especially since I manifest most of it before the year is even close to being over. I record it and listen to it several times a day. This is extremely POWERFUL!

My Daily Affirmation:

I make a list of the goals I want to accomplish and turn them into affirmations. I review this list on a weekly basis. I always start them with I AM, as these two words are the most powerful words. Not only do I write them down but I record them on my phone and laptop and listen to them, along with the recording of my future letter. I listen to them when I first wake up, before going to bed, and when I go for my mini power walks.

Here is an example of powerful daily affirmations to use:

I AM beautiful. I AM abundant. I AM a successful business owner. I AM joy. I AM healthy. I AM financially free. I AM happy. I AM vibrant. I AM sexy. I AM successful. I AM worthy of accomplishing everything that I want to manifest. I AM energetic. I AM in the best shape of my life. I AM love. I AM an amazing wife. I AM Zen. Etc…

Take the time right now to do your I AM affirmations. Please personalize it and use what resonates with you—and add more if you need or want to. Watch the shift in your energy levels and enjoy manifesting amazing things.

Being grateful:

Every day before going to sleep, I write in my gratefulness journal everything that I am grateful for that day. At first, this may be really hard for you to do. But start with naming five things you are grateful for. It could be as simple as: I am grateful that I woke up breathing this morning, that someone smiled at me today, that I made someone smile, that I woke up to the birds singing, that I had enough food to eat today, that I had a great conversation with a friend, that the sun was shining today, etc…

When you are being grateful, you manifest and attract a lot of good things into your life—as you are engulfed in a super positive energy. When I am going through a tough time, I go through my gratefulness journal and realize how blessed I truly am. It helps to shift my focus on the positive, and I start to attract positive things/persons/situations again into my life.

Meditation:

I always block off at least twenty minutes in the first hour I'm awake to meditate and give myself an energy healing session. Meditation is very powerful in helping to not only manifest what you want but also to stay aligned with your true self. I also visualize what it is I want to manifest when I meditate. It is a very powerful time for me and one of my favorite times of day, because it allows me to be in quiet and focus on *me*. It is very important to meditate—it allows you to remain true to yourself. When you are true to yourself, you have the ability to manifest quicker and bigger things.

Surround yourself with uplifting and positive people:

The five people that you surround yourself with will determine who you are. So choose wisely. Choose people who reflect whom you want to be like. Choose people who will uplift you and believe in you. It is better to have a small circle of close friends than to have hundreds of fake friends. I even like to say that it is better to be alone than with the energy suckers. I re-evaluate my inner circle on a daily basis and it has changed my life.

Daily Ritual Schedule:

I have a daily ritual schedule to keep me focused. Within the first hour of waking up, I count my blessings and say thank you to the Universe for the amazing day ahead of me. I also listen to my future letter and affirmations and then meditate and have an energy healing session for at least twenty minutes. I then look at my vision boards on the wall next to my bed. I always have a big smile when I do this, even if my life is in shambles. Why? Because it helps to shift my energy and helps me focus on the positive so I will attract more positive in my life.

I also make sure to listen to my future letter and affirmations several times a day. When I go for my power walks, I listen to them. Anytime I take a break or go to the washroom, I will listen to them. And I always listen to them before I go to sleep.

One of the last things that I do before going to sleep is to write in my journal everything I am grateful for that day. I also write my affirmations in this journal. I look at my vision board and visualize that I already have everything on it.

I also make a point to go for nature walks several times a week to help keep me grounded.

Do I always follow my daily rituals? No. I am human, after all. I feel it when I haven't done them, as I start attracting negative things in my life and become miserable because nothing is going the way I consciously want it to go.

When I do follow my daily rituals, I manifest the most amazing things into my life.

Always remember that there is enough ABUNDANCE for everyone. You can MANIFEST anything you want. You need to start by ASKING for it! BELIEVE it will happen, and RECEIVE it when it comes to you! You DESERVE to have anything you truly want!

If my chapter has resonated with you, please do not hesitate to reach out to me. I would love to hear your feedback, struggles, and successes.

Happy MANIFESTING!

LISA NESSER

Lisa Nesser has been living and working with Burmese/Myanmar refugees and minority groups in Thailand for the last ten years. She founded Thai Freedom House—a community language and arts learning center which provides free classes, seven days a week, to vulnerable populations that have nowhere else to turn. Volunteers from all over the world come to intern and volunteer at Thai Freedom House where she serves as a mentor. Her vegetarian charity café, Free Bird Café, is highly successful with visitors both local and international coming to taste the delicious ethnic food and support the cause.

🏠 www.thaifreedomhouse.org

✉ lisa@thaifreedomhouse.org

in th.linkedin.com/pub/lisa-nesser/a1/256/763

f www.facebook.com/thaifreedomhousecm

f www.facebook.com/freebirdcafe

🐦 www.twitter.com/FreeBirdCafe

📌 www.pinterest.com/freebirdcafe/

📷 @freebirdcafe #thaifreedomhouse

MANIFESTATION 9

$\mathcal{H}$OW TO CREATE THE SPACE AROUND YOU FOR MANIFESTING

By Lisa Nesser

I manifested *this* opportunity! I consciously manifested an opportunity to write for publication...just a few days before I was invited to be included in this book. Let me tell you my story of how I got to where I am as the founder of the organization of my dreams and how things started changing dramatically for me when I began thinking about manifesting. Yes, manifesting—that is, not just *thinking* about the process of putting into the Universe what you believe you want or need, but actually *creating* a SPACE in your life for that to happen.

Having always been intrigued by the concept of having faith and the rituals of various religions, I took Eastern religion classes at university and eventually got involved in the *Students for a Free Tibet* organization. Drawn to the Tibetans' struggle, I traveled to a remote refugee camp in India to observe their culture firsthand and offered my services, primarily as a documentary photographer. At the end of my first stint volunteering with the monks, it became apparent that I was most useful there as an English teacher, enabling refugees to share their own stories with the world. I had no concept of manifestation at this point, I just knew I was living my life with the most pure and positive intentions as possible to help others, while fueling my desire to experience humanity and faith.

When I returned to the states, I started a new course of study—education. During the next two years, I made several trips back to India, working with the Tibetan monks, teaching and establishing relationships in the community. One of the friendships I developed was with a young monk about my age. He taught me about Buddhism through his daily example of living a life of pure devotion. I was surrounded by ritual, prayer, and mantras, and everyone around me was manifesting their future incarnation by their present actions. But it was one lesson in particular this monk taught me that has stayed with me. He told me that every morning before he prayed or prepared tea for his teacher, the first thing he did was sweep his room. He explained that by starting his day with the sweeping, he was not only clearing out any dust or dirt in the room but clearing the cluttering of his mind—the worries, doubts, or thoughts from the day before that may be troubling him. That simple yet powerful lesson struck a chord with me and has stayed with me until now.

Eventually, my life led me to open Thai Freedom House in 2005—a community learning center for Burmese refugees in Thailand. We have provided essential education, emergency assistance, clothing, shelter, and support to thousands of people since then. The only regular financial support we have had is that of our social enterprise, Free Bird Café, which I opened in 2009, located in Chiang Mai, Thailand, it serves healthy, local vegetarian cuisine. I lived and worked within the community learning center from its inception. Although I have volunteers from all over the world who come to support the project, and our own students who volunteer as interns, the responsibility for the success of the project weighs heavily on my shoulders. I am the one who develops the community outreach projects, provides crisis management to our families, guides the values and culture of the organization, trains and mentors the volunteers, and strives to find funding to keep it going every month so we don't leave our fifty families and extended community without services.

As the students thrived and succeeded at Thai Freedom House, programs flourished, and the project gained respect in the community, I became ill. My habit of internalizing all the stress and responsibility of running such an operation alone meant I woke up every morning in a panic, fearing today would be the day it all fell apart. I realized I needed to change my environment and my approach to our problems. I finally understood it was the stress and worry that was causing my sickness, and no matter how much I fretted all month, we had always found a way to pay the bills and survive. I wondered if maybe we could achieve the same results without all the stress and worry.

In November of 2013, I decided to move out of my community learning center. I was tired of not having any personal space and always being at work. I had been thinking about it for months but was afraid I wouldn't be able to afford it—my mindset had blocked me from finding a space. When I decided that I WAS going to move out, and that it would work out no matter what, I found a house to rent in a perfect location very quickly. I moved in, decorated, and organized my new home. I immediately started sleeping soundly and was waking up with a smile on my face every morning! I finally had my own space!

With my newfound clarity, I began to think again about manifestation. I reflected on what the young monk had said to me in India and how I could actually create a space for manifestation to happen by simple actions. My thoughts turned to how I had struggled the last few years trying to keep my head above water and keep my organization afloat. I had been terrified, which paralyzed me in the same space, every day, without being able to move forward. I had lost my faith. What I needed to do was start to actually BELIEVE everything would be all right.

I needed a plan. I had long believed in natural healing techniques, such as using crystals, tinctures, Reiki, meditation, nutrition, and essential oils, but I needed to widen my approach. I decided to treat my entire home as an entity, a pulsing energy that was affecting me physically and mentally. I began to prepare my space every day as a positive environment to heal and nurture my body and mind. That's when I developed the following rules for creating a magical space for manifestation. Try these simple steps to create your own space and watch your dreams unfold:

1. Esthetics – Carefully observe your living and working space—are the colors doing what they can to energize, calm, sooth, or cheer you up? Think about what you need to achieve in every area of your house or work space and decorate according to that need. Research color therapy and choose colors that feel right for you.

2. Clutter – Remove things that block the flow of energy in your home. You may want to look into Feng Shui as a guide, or simply look around. Is there clutter and piles of things that are unorganized and just holding space? Imagine energy flowing through your home as a stream of water—are there dams stopping it up? Experiment with moving your furniture around. Get all the way down to your closets and that junk drawer where everything is tossed. Look under your bed and in your basement. Many people use these spaces as "storage" but those are the spaces that should be clear of clutter. Items hold energy, so be aware of what you are surrounding yourself with.

3. Scent – Have you ever noticed how scents can take you right to a particular space and time? Scent is a powerful tool for controlling our physical and mental space. Avoid artificial chemical scents and consider a simple essential oil diffuser instead. You can make little sachets of essential oil mixes to place around your house. I have groups of oils in respective areas of my house where I might need them. Fennel and peppermint in the kitchen; tea tree in the bathroom; frankincense and lavender in the bedroom; and a sage spray in my living space. Every morning I anoint my chakras with intention of activating the energy in my body and then I diffuse or spray what oils I feel I need according to what I am working on that day.

4. Sound – Words are powerful, so are sounds. There is a reason that mantras have been a part of ancient religions for centuries. Hinduism and Buddhism both use mantras as a devotional tool. I use them to charge my space with intention every day. When I wake up in the morning, I turn on a playlist of mantras and melodies to set the vibration in my space.

When I took control of my space, everything started to happen. My body started to heal, donations came into my charity project like never before, my students gained widespread recognition for their progress, and obstacles that had long stood in the way to our success disappeared. There was now SPACE for success—a space I had been blocking before with my anxiety and worry. I urge you to create your own space. Try these techniques and please let me know how it works for you.

LIL LEZARRE

Lil let her heart guide her and is now living her dream life as an entrepreneur. She is a three-time best-selling international co-author, and public speaker. She has her own business that she started from scratch part-time and is building a franchise corporation—all this from following her passions. She knows firsthand the incredible power of manifesting and shares some of her lessons with you. "I am honored to be part of this book—Christine's first book, *Success in High Heels*, opened my eyes to the possibilities of living the life of an entrepreneur. Now to have a chapter in this sequel is a living testament to what's available to you when you manifest it."

- ✉ Lil.lezarre@gmail.com
- ⌂ www.lillezarre.com
- ⌂ www.tenderlovingcups.com
- f www.facebook.com/pages/Tender-Loving-Cups/215675105173124
- 🐦 @LilsProBraFitN

MANIFESTATION 10

THE KEYS TO MANIFESTING YOUR DREAMS

By Lil Lezarre

It's important to recognize, whether you are conscious of it or not, that you have a belief system that guides and governs your thoughts, words, and actions. It may be rooted in religion—ethnocentric or secular monotheistic, whatever resonates with you—there is no right or wrong answer. Every one of us has our reason and it's right for us. When I say resonates, it's a RIGHT feeling you get deep inside, and your body understands it. Belief is more than just saying it—the saying "Believe with your heart and your soul" is very accurate, as you have to feel it deeply.

I'm a firm believer that we were put on this earth with a purpose, and when you discover your dream or purpose and you pursue it, life becomes amazing. Our bodies tell us what our purpose is. It will be something you have a natural talent for and you enjoy doing—it fulfills you. You may have to think back to your childhood. What put a smile on your face? What did you yearn to do? Start exploring what YOU like.

Remember, this is about you and what you feel inside—not what you've been told that you like or are good at, or what's best for you. What does your heart tell you? What desire have you always had deep down inside? What activity has always sparked your interest but you assumed you wouldn't be good at so you never tried? Discovering yourself is a process in itself but it's the first step to realizing your dream, and it's a step you must complete before living your dream life. You cannot have success on the *outside* without success on the *inside*. Yes, you can make a lot of money, but money is *nothing* when you have that hole on the inside. If you have that feeling something is missing, you haven't achieved success on the *inside* yet.

My road to discovering my purpose started in 2013 when I attended a book signing with Lisa Kroeger for *Unmask the Liar*, a step-by-step on how to leave an abusive relationship. I mentioned to Lisa that I'd like to share my story if she ever wrote a book about how great life is after leaving an abusive relationship. She put me in touch with Kate Gardner, and I signed up for Kate's *The Missing Piece – A Transformational Journey* book. Next, I read Christine Marmoy's book, *Success in High Heels*, and that resonated with me like nothing I've ever experienced before. In October 2013, I flew to Ireland to attend her seminar, "These Dreams Are Made for Walking." It was the weirdest thing, because I didn't even question my gut feeling that I *had* to attend her seminar. I'm not a traveller—in fact that was only the second time I'd been out of Canada. I didn't even know what the seminar was about – only that I had to go. At Christine's seminar, I met Kate Gardner in person and started working with Kate as my life coach, and that's when I started digging deep inside to discover my dream.

We have so many ingrained beliefs that keep us stuck. For example, removing toxic people from your life—this is especially hard if it's family, because we have the belief that family is of ultimate importance (blood is thicker than water). Don't misquote me, family is very important, but I'm talking about the family members that are toxic, and the only reason you associate with them is because you've been told it's the right thing to do. There are situations where you are better off without them. If your only tie is that you're related, you do have a *choice*. Negative people do not support you. They will have you questioning your ideas, creating more self-doubt, and you will find yourself staying stuck, always finding an excuse or reason not to pursue your dream. We have plenty of limiting beliefs, negative self-talk, and the big surprise—fears. They're a surprise because they're everywhere and when you realize it's a fear that's holding you back, you push through it and the other side kicks ass. It gives you more confidence; you have more self-respect. You can't do this alone and that's why it's so important that you surround yourself with positive and supportive people. They keep you in the positive circle and you keep going up—this is one of the most important changes you will make to living the life of your dreams. There are still times those fears sneak up and they do grab you, but being able to recognize them enables you to bulldoze your way through them—and once again, you've grown. Surrounding yourself with supportive people also helps you push beyond your comfort zone, and that's a really *tough* zone. Our body's nature is to protect us, and when the conscious mind is telling it we're not safe (i.e., fear), we start feeling anxiety and the easy way out is to stop. That's why so many people stay stuck—it's easier.

A mindset change makes a huge difference in how you approach a situation. How many times do you experience a particular scenario repeating itself? You know how the circumstance is going to end because the same thing happens every time. A simple mindset change from "This happens all the time" to "What can I do to make the situation better?" Go ahead and try this. Ask yourself, "What can I do to make the situation better?" You'll be surprised how many little things annoy us, but we've accustomed ourselves to accept the situation instead of doing something to change it. This is just one of many mindset changes I've discovered—it makes life so much less dramatic and more enjoyable.

Investing in yourself always gives you a rate of return that you can't put a dollar value on. Growth is a nonstop process and we all need guidance—even coaches need coaches. They help you gain clarity, stay focused on your dreams, keep you accountable, and open your eyes to opportunities around you. You may have to try a few coaches or mentors before finding the one that clicks with you, but it's important to find the right one. You have to be comfortable enough to be completely honest with them and make sure they hold the same values and vision as you do. Take courses to improve your skills. Think outside the box. I know a lady who even took singing lessons to improve her voice for public speaking.

In February 2014, I left my fulltime job to take my part-time bra business on full time and build it into a global franchise opportunity. Leaving the security of a regular paycheck wasn't easy, but becoming an entrepreneur was one of the best decisions of my life. Lots of work goes into everything, but when you love what you're doing and it feels right inside, it doesn't feel like work. Being able to do as your body feels allows you to accomplish so much more, and it's so much easier. When you have the inspiration, you can focus on something and things simply flow. The more you're *enjoying* everything you do, the less you *work*. Another huge thing for me is being able to live by my values. In my personal life, I've lived by my values but I was not always able to at work—now I can apply my values to every area of my life.

I am manifesting my life of dreams, and doors of opportunity are continually opening for me. Finding my purpose—to inspire and empower women's and men's fulfillment through respect, authenticity, honesty, and gratitude—has removed that empty feeling inside. I get to help women and men make their life better by providing properly fitting affordable quality bras. I make sure my values are the standard in my franchise. Life is great—I'm living the life of my dreams. You can live your life of dreams too—that's why we are here. Take that first step. Discover yourself—you will be amazed at what you can do.

KENDRA R. GAINEY

Kendra R. Gainey is an entrepreneur extraordinaire whose passion is to inspire women to Dare2Own! She is the proprietor and CEO of Gainey Girl Boutique, LLC, a women's specialty clothing store; and Angel Care, A Family Child Care Place, LLC. Kendra lives to inspire, encourage, and empower women to turn their hobbies into businesses that provide financial relief and stability. She believes each woman is just one step away from reaching her true potential. Kendra lives in New Jersey with her husband, Bo, and daughter.

🏠 www.GaineyGirlBoutique.com

f www.facebook.com/gaineygirlboutique

🐦 www.twitter.com/GaineyGirl216

MANIFESTATION 11

STAY THE COURSE—
EVEN WHEN IT CHANGES

By Kendra R. Gainey

It was March 2013. Spring was in bloom. Everything was coming alive and the cold, harsh winter weather was but a memory. I was excited my business partner and I had just signed a two-year lease for what would become our very first commercial retail space. So many decisions and choices to make—fixtures, layout, color scheme, lighting, signage, new marketing material, phone lines, Internet—the list went on and on. I couldn't sleep—I was overfilled with the joy of it all. The contractor had already been hired and the grand opening was set for Saturday, June 22, 2013.

The next three months were filled with cleanup, painting, deliveries, putting things together, installing equipment, setting up displays, anticipation, gratefulness, thankfulness, and some challenges—things were clearly changing. But what was once a dream was slowly turning into a nightmare, and we hadn't even opened. I held fast to what I knew to be true—Romans 8:28 (KJV): "And we know that all things work together for good to them that love God, to them who are called according to his purpose."

The boutique was more than just a place to sell and buy clothing and accessories. It was a ministry—a place where I could showcase and share God's love, daily, with all kinds of people. So I couldn't allow the enemy or his devices to distract me. I had to remain focused and tied to my purpose. I had Kingdom work to do. My faith sustained me and justified me.

My advice to anyone who may be in the midst of such a situation is to remember your vision (dream) started with you, but it really is much bigger than *you*. What you have to offer has the power and authority to affect and change lives. That's why you're being pressed on every side. My mother use to say to me in times of trouble, "Take it with a grain of salt." What she meant is that whatever *it* was, in the scheme of things, it's a small thing—so there's no need to get bent out of shape. You have to remember what will be at stake if you respond to negativity with negativity. It makes your journey longer and reaching your destination longer and more difficult. So, stay the course…God is your compass.

WISDOM PEARL: WHEN FACING ADVERSITY, GIVE WAY TO HUMBLENESS.

Rule #1 – Hold fast to what is good and true. As the storm begins to blow, brace for it. In realizing your dream(s), you will encounter many challenges, roadblocks, and distractions, but hold fast to what is good and true—don't give in to temptation.

There will be no eye for an eye in this battle if you plan to win the war. These encounters will only be teachable moments that will prepare you for your next level.

Remember, you are VICTORIOUS!

The boutique's time was drawing near. All the work was done, the sign hung, the displays in place, the merchandise looked good—overall, I felt great. The boutique was opening the very next day. Friends and family from near and far had given their RSVP. We would all gather to celebrate the opening of Gainey Girl Boutique. As I stood outside, the grand opening sign was swaying back and forth in the wind. I stood back to take it all in. Wow, I felt accomplished and thankful as I headed home to rest for the big day.

The next day was "grand opening" day. It was finally happening. I couldn't have been happier. I had friends helping to man the vital positions of the day, so I was free to greet and chat with everyone. The continuous sound of the cash register ringing, ringing, ringing, and ringing again gave me great hope. I was truly grateful and prayers and blessings filled the Boutique. At 9 p.m., the last customer left. I'd been at it since 10 a.m. that morning, but I wasn't tired. Ah, the joy of ownership. There was no turning back.

Fall approached. The business was steadily but slowly growing—but the partnership was dying. Outwardly, it looked like two women working together, aligned on the same path, but that wasn't the reality. Something had happened. I wasn't sure what, but every day brought something new. It was getting difficult and burdensome to navigate someone else's constantly-changing moods. I was trying to build a brand, and it deserved every bit of me—and that's just what I planned to give. Though life was changing right before my eyes, I chose to swim *with the current*, enjoying the lift. Life happens when we learn to shift.

WISDOM PEARL: NEVER LET THE ACTIONS OF ANOTHER DETERMINE YOUR ACTIONS.

Rule #2 – Don't lose yourself in someone else's fight. At any given time, people are going through life—that means we all are subject to frustrations, let downs, facing fears, childhood disappointments, self-inflicted issues, low self-esteem, the baggage of yesteryear, and dare I say, even envy. Some people, no matter how good their intentions are, are self-sabotaging. Beware.

Remember, you are VICTORIOUS!

As time went on, the temperature was getting colder—and I don't mean the weather. I had to remind myself constantly that God had a plan for me and that my journey had a destination. I refused to lose myself in someone else's fight, so I encouraged myself with Jeremiah 29:11 (KJV): "For I know the thoughts that I think toward you, saith the Lord, thoughts of peace, and not of evil, to give you an expected end."

December 2013—the end was near. I'd just had two charges filed against me. They were bogus and unfounded. And it's such a shame that that kind of nonsense clutters our court system. Nevertheless, it wasn't my fight. I could see the breaking of day, which meant there was still hope. Our court date was in January 2014. I didn't plan to fight but I was going to defend myself. But what do you know? The charges were dropped. The important business at hand became dissolving the partnership that was beyond repair. It wasn't good for the growth of the business and we were headed in two different directions. We had a binding lease. I was torn. Should I concede? What price was I willing to pay to be free? Should I have to pay any price? That's where I struggled to make my decision, because I felt like conceding meant I'd lost. But, ultimately, the truth is that by conceding, I had won.

March 2014 and I was now the sole owner of the boutique. I was enjoying ownership and the business was growing steadily. The Gainey Girl Boutique brand even included its own signature scent candles and our private bath and body collection. Opportunities to grow as a speaker and author increased every day. What a difference a year made. The trials and trouble of yesteryear were a distant memory, and I had my *happy* back—that alone is priceless.

WISDOM PEARL: YOU'RE PREDESTINED TO WIN. DON'T GIVE UP. DON'T QUIT. PUSH FORWARD.

Rule#3 – Above all, remain true to you. As we stride toward fulfillment in business, at home, in our careers, and in life in general, remember that the best way to enjoy a life of fulfillment is to live a life of service. No matter what challenges or obstacles you come up against, be ready in an instant to share what you know, help where you can, and encourage always. As you give, you are positioned to receive.

Remember, you are VICTORIOUS!

My advice to you is to know yourself, what you stand for, and what your purpose is. Then be committed to embarking on your journey and remembering you have a destination. You might start your journey out with someone, but along the way, your purpose may pull you in another direction—and you have to be OK with that. Have your three guiding rules that you refuse to compromise on. Rules that will help to center you when the storm is raging or situations become difficult. Have personal wisdom pearls that encourage you and focus you. Wisdom pearls should remind the outer man what the spirit man knows to be true.

As I continue to be true to my three rules every day, I see growth in all areas of my life. The rules have helped me hold myself accountable when I wanted to let go, which in turn has allowed me to flourish in areas that surprise me. I didn't invent the wheel, but I have improved it and fashioned it to fit me. You too can do the same thing in this world of sharing. It's easy once you understand who you are, what you stand for, and what your purpose is. Then you can build and borrow—it's OK.

The key to manifesting all that you want in your life is directly connected to what you feed yourself, sprinkled with hard work and perseverance. Stay the course, even if it changes. Don't give up and don't quit—keep pushing forward.

Remember, you are VICTORIOUS!

Wisdom Pearl: "Success isn't just about what you accomplish in your life, it's about what you INSPIRE others to do."
—Unknown

BARBARA BOXWELL

I am a therapeutic massage therapist specializing in myofascial release therapy and craniosacral therapy. I help bring pain relief to people who cannot get relief through conventional methods.

I am passionate about giving hope to those people who have lost hope or have given up because they don't know about alternative methods that have the potential to help their bodies heal themselves.

I have spoken and continue to speak to groups about clinical research and case studies that indicate positive results for muscle weakness and other chronic conditions.

For further information, contact me at:

✉ bpboxwell@juno.com

f www.facebook.com/midlandmfr

🐦 www.twitter.com/MidlandMFR

MANIFESTATION 12

ℱROM CHAOS AND FATIGUE TO DOLPHIN HEALING

By Barbara Boxwell

After ten years of running my family's manufacturing business, taking care of my mom, two houses, and two dogs, playing music and being involved with church work, I was exhausted and burned out. In 2005, we sold the family business at a loss, and it took until 2012 for the final dissolution and disposition.

Cleaning out a business is not easy—there are files and papers and artifacts that need to be kept for years afterward. These were kept in storage, along with many other pieces of historical significance from my parents. At that point in my life, I had two storage units, two houses, two dogs, my music, my church work, and my mom to take care of and, very importantly, no job.

Prior to assuming the running of the business after my father's death, I taught accounting and business classes at the collegiate level as an associate professor of accounting. However, I was tired of the pace of the business world. The economy was at a low point and I knew that there were no full-time positions at any nearby area colleges to continue teaching; I began looking for another career that would be more gentle, rewarding, and fulfilling.

My bachelor's degree was in biology and chemistry, and I had always been interested in alternative health. I'd been going to a massage therapist for the ten years I ran the family business and had received good results for de-stressing. So I found a massage school that fit my schedule and finances, enrolled, and became certified in therapeutic massage. (Note that at the point of my writing this, my home state has created a licensure program for massage therapists, and I am now a licensed massage therapist.)

In September of 2006, I opened my own massage business and went back to teaching accounting as an adjunct instructor for two local universities. The teaching provided supplemental income while the massage business grew.

My massage business flourished and reached a load of about twenty clients per month. At that point, I learned that I could not focus on these two different areas of my life and remain true to myself. Teaching required a more left-brained, methodical, task-oriented, guarded focus while therapeutic massage required a more right-brained, intuitive, open-hearted approach. To go from one to the other, particularly on the same day, became difficult.

I have been looking at different spiritual practices most of my life— trying them to see what is a best fit for me. Prayer focuses on asking God for something that would make your life better than it is now. Meditation isn't asking but listening for direction. I seemed to be waiting for some external force to make it better for me or to give some specific direction I could obey. The various methods I tried seemed to be external to my own selfhood.

Then I realized that perhaps the answer lay inside me. The only way I could get to that place was to be still and reach for the "calm" that lay in the depths of my being. So I began to take time to *be still* and *get calm*. The less I did, the more clear I became.

Getting calm and being still remained a challenge. I used many techniques. Sometimes it was meditating, sometimes listening to music, other times it was reading an inspirational passage from one of several books, or listening to a recording of a guided meditation. I was seeking the still, small voice from my soul for the answers.

My focus in my therapeutic massage business is on facilitating the client's body to relax enough for it to heal itself. I use techniques of myofascial release on the fascial-muscle tissues and craniosacral therapy for fluid movement within the body.

In myofascial release, the therapist engages with the client's muscles and acts as a support for them, gently persuading the fascial tissue to release the restrictions and unwind. In craniosacral therapy, we go one step further. We are constantly listening to the client's body to detect significant rhythms or lack of rhythms. In either case, techniques of listening, getting quiet, and being calm are the same techniques I use to find direction in my life and in my business. These modalities are similar to my own personal philosophy, which is to become more authentic and true to myself.

I slowly realized as I was helping to assist others in their own healing, I was healing, too. It is a priority in my life that I become healthy in mind, body, and spirit. "Without my own physical, emotional, and spiritual health, I can do nothing" has become my mantra.

I continued to take extra courses in both myofascial release therapy and craniosacral therapy. The more classes I took, the more I could connect with new clients. Because I had chosen to take my social security benefits early, I thought I should only make a certain amount of money annually. That was incorrect thinking. One day, while listening to that internal "small voice," I changed my mind and decided to make as much money as I could and take as many classes as I could to gear up for building my business even further.

This decision seemed to be pleasing to the universe, and in 2013, I manifested more clients than I ever thought possible. I took classes that became the basis for my next adventure in healing. Soon, I will be swimming with the dolphins in the Bahamas while taking the bio-aquatic exploration class. This class will give me the opportunity to participle in dolphin-assisted therapy, where the dolphins assist in my own therapy and healing.

This adventure is a dream come true. It is something I have thought about for a long time. I even have childhood memories of being intrigued about dolphins when I listened to my dad explain how intelligent these beings were. Current reading has opened up a new world to me about the history of dolphins and the mythology and science of their healing powers.

This year, I have put aside my fears and worries regarding money and have begun to de-clutter my physical surroundings—including the storage units. What a wonderful experience this is! The units are empty and my home life is in control. This has given me new life and has been a breath of fresh air. When I am in need of money, I ask the Universe—and, within hours, a new client will call or I'll hear from a client I haven't seen in a while who wants to schedule an appointment. I feel totally supported as I continue to hone my listening skills in all areas of my life.

I am grateful to the Universe for my therapeutic massage business, which continues to thrive, as well as the various opportunities that occur to help me grow more comfortable with my true self. I am feeling very supported on the journey I've taken to find my true work and my true self. It's happening!

As an epilogue, I would share that my mother passed away in December of 2007 and I now have only one dog, Chester, who is a wonderful companion. Those two storage units have been emptied and the contents have found their best homes. I no longer need to take on adjunct college classes for supplemental income, and I'm entirely grateful that my craniosacral and myofascial release massage therapy business has reached a point of total financial support for me.

I have truly moved beyond the point of "chaos and fatigue"—from doing what I thought the world expected of me as a responsible human being to a profession where I am able to facilitate healing while also being healed. What a marvelous gift from the Universe!

The best advice I can give to my readers is this: be true to yourself. Find out what gives you the most internal, lasting pleasure, ask for guidance, and then listen to what the Universe is telling you. And most importantly, follow your heart.

ANGELLA JOHNSON

Angella Johnson is a business visionary and a marketing and messaging strategist with an intuitive flair. She is the secret weapon behind conscious businesses that are committed to changing the world and making great money.

After building her business twice to six figures, Angella discovered that following her intuition and truth—rather than following someone else's one-size-fits-all formula —created the most joy, financial abundance, and freedom. She combines strategy and intuition to help other SOULpreneurs and businesses integrate all their gifts with their big vision so they can be the contribution they desire and live a powerful and prosperous life they love.

To debunk the success myths and bridge the gap from your purpose to your profits, get instant access to the free training series, "Intuitive Business—Real Money." Learn the secrets (without the fluff or hype) to make more money, have more joy, and fulfill your purpose.

🏠 www.SoulVisionBusinessSchool.com

🏠 www.AngellaJohnson.com

✉ angella@angellajohnson.com

f www.facebook.com/SoulVisionStrategies

🐦 www.twitter.com/soulvisionbiz

📌 www.pinterest.com/soulpreneur

MANIFESTATION 13

DRESS FOR SUCCESS: YOGA PANTS AND A T-SHIRT (WITHOUT A BRA)

By Angella Johnson

People have a vision of what success looks like: beautifully branded websites and professional headshots with perfect lighting, hair, and makeup.

Behind the curtain, success is raw, real, and not as pretty. You can typically find me in my home office in yoga pants, a T-shirt, and on a good day, I even wear a bra. So how have I created a six-figure business and helped thousands of people, both private clients and those who attend my events? It comes down to these four words:

What do you want?

In 2012, this was the question I didn't know how to answer. I knew I had to answer it soon, because I was depressed and didn't like my business.

I followed someone else's formula to build my six-figure business and I was shocked to find that a side of joy and purpose didn't come with the main course of six figures.

I followed advice from experts and colleagues that I should ONLY focus on money and marketing as my main message. The result? I abandoned my intuition and spirituality. In short, I abandoned myself. Since I've been highly intuitive my whole life, I was miserable.

When I honestly answered the simple question, "What do I want?" I was scared by the truth bomb that emerged. I finally got quiet and listened to my soul's whisper; I was guided to come out of the spiritual closet MY way.

The idea of creating a community of SOULpreneurs was born and I knew that my business would change forever. So, what is a SOULpreneur? (I'm glad you asked.)

soul•pre•neur [sohl-pruh-nur]

noun

1. Spiritual entrepreneur who fully expresses their *soul* purpose and intuition without apology.

2. Business owner who expands the economy by empowering lives *and* creating financial wealth.

3. Transformation agent who is crazy enough to know they can change the world, so they do.

The biggest catalyst to rebuild my business back to six figures — after I completely disassembled it—was this very simple question: What do you want?

I've asked thousands of women this question and the majority of them answer it with the mindset of what they *think* they can get based on their history and beliefs about themselves. Answering this simple question with that energy will squash your soul's vision and true desires *every single time*. It will always negate what you really want and you will get stuck in cycles of people-pleasing, ignoring your intuition, and spending months (or even years) and thousands of dollars experimenting and spinning in circles. Not knowing what you want is the recipe for disaster.

Take a moment right now and write down what you really want. Do this every day and you'll get to your soul's big vision (or *soul vision*). This process is simple, yet the breakthroughs will be profound; everything is at stake and everything can change.

This exercise is NOT what you want for your kids, spouse, clients, or even the world. This is not the time to be altruistic or go with what you think you SHOULD want, or what you think others want for you. It's what YOU want. Be selfish. Be materialistic. Be crazy. Get those layers out of you and you will sink into your deepest desires, which is where the magic happens. The clarity will activate the Universe to bring it to you.

The first time I did this exercise, I wrote down that I wanted a pair of $900.00 shoes. Why? I met a woman at an event who talked about how, with her business success, she could "now buy a $900.00 pair of shoes", as she pointed down to her elegant yet bold foot attire. I was envious and inspired at the same time. I thought I wanted $900.00 shoes.

Guess what? After asking myself what I really wanted every single day for several weeks, I realized I didn't want the shoes. I would rather spend $900.00 toward a trip to Italy, or art for my home. Most of all, I wanted freedom.

Freedom is doing what I want, when I want, how I want, with whom I want. This activated my "money gateways" in my business, and I've never looked back—all because of one small question I was brave enough to answer honestly.

When I realized I had to do business differently, I let go of most of my clients, mentors, and other people in my life who didn't align with my truth. I blew up my business and rebuilt it from the ground up. Every day I was scared, but with the alternative being to let my soul die, I knew the only option was to do it *scared*. I knew how it felt to let my soul die, and I was never going back to that.

How did I rebuild my six-figure business to the one that I now LOVE? How do I guide my clients and tribe to embrace building a business with their intuition fully intact and making real money? Let me tell you how.

These manifesting rituals will set you free:

1. Know what you want.

Be unwavering in what you want, while you dance with divine timing and receive pleasant surprises.

2. Speak up and tell the truth faster.

Simply put, you say *yes* when you mean yes, and you say *no* when you mean no.

This also means honoring what you really want in your business, including who you really want to serve, how you want to serve them (your products and programs), and your pricing. It takes courage to turn away non-ideal clients and to charge premium pricing. Go for it!

A side bonus is you stop being so people-pleasing (boring!) in your message and you actually put your stake in the ground. You draw your line in the sand and declare what you want to do and how you want to do it. You do what you are a genius at and not just what you think might make you money.

You honor your intuition and don't talk yourself into things that don't light you up.

You hold yourself and your clients to a level of accountability that creates breakthroughs and results because you aren't trying to appease them, but you tell the truth, even when it's uncomfortable. This doesn't make you popular at times, but consider this: telling the truth is unconditional love.

3. Stop apologizing.

Ladies, we've got to STOP apologizing. Listen to your conversations and listen to other women and you'll see what I mean.

"I'm sorry, but can you tell me the time?"

"I'm sorry, can I borrow a pen?"

"I'm sorry, but I think this is a good idea…"

Only say *sorry* when you have actually done something that deserves an apology.

Saying sorry in a meaningless fashion is like apologizing for taking up space in the world and since YOU have a big role in the world, you better start getting comfortable.

Another thing—please, please stop apologizing for your body. Your thighs are perfect. Your crow's feet around your eyes show how many times you've smiled with joy—and that is *beautiful*. Love your body *now*. The world needs all of you, not just the parts the media portrays as acceptable.

4. Show gratitude while honoring your desires.

Gratitude is a path to freedom. Gratitude can also put you into complacency and stagnation faster than a New York minute.

Share your authentic gratitude daily, in fact, every hour.

However, when something is NOT working for you, don't override that realization by claiming things like, "It's OK, at least I have ____," or "All is well…see all of the other blessings I have in my life?"

You have every right to want what you want and be in the environment that supports your desires. Accept anything less than that, and you deny your divinity. Since abundance is part of your divinity, you shut off money flow every time you override your desires with accepting something less than what you truly want.

5. Do it scared.

A common message that comes through the intuitive work I do with my clients is to do something that scares you every single day.

If you are waiting to FEEL awesome all the time, before you jump into the life of your dreams, you will wait forever.

Life is happening now. Use the fear to fuel your quantum leaps.

6. Be vulnerable.

Breakdowns are inevitable. Trying to get through them alone will take you much longer than necessary.

You don't need to suffer to prove you are strong. You are strong because you are divine; embrace it.

Pretending that you have it all together will not get you anywhere. Show the world the real you. Reach out to people who will be honest with you and love you at the same time. Someone who sees you in your greatness will support you during the breakdowns, so you can get to the breakthrough quicker.

Authenticity is the new business currency; show the real you.

Living these six principles will exponentially activate your manifesting power.

Lastly, remember this: You are right on time. You are not a second late for the life of your dreams. But you have to *show up*.

POLLY HADFIELD

An administrator with an entrepreneurial spirit, and more than thirty years' experience, Polly Hadfield has led and trained successful teams in both the administrative arena and network marketing. Polly and her husband run a successful home-based public adjusting business, which educates property owners about their insurance policies and, in the event of a covered loss, assists them in obtaining their full entitlement. They have built their business on integrity, hard work, and respect.

🏠 www.metropa.com/kenandpolly

✉ pollymetropa@gmail.com

in www.linkedin.com/in/pollyhadfield/

🐦 www.twitter.com/pollyhadfield

f www.facebook.com/pollyhadfield

MANIFESTATION 14

Manifest to be your best

By Polly Hadfield

If you're happy and you know it...

Have you ever wondered how some people wake up happy, vibrant, and full of life?

We all know people like this. They are energetic, productive, confident, and passionate. They go through the day with a positive aura around them. And no matter what happens, nothing seems to faze them. People are naturally drawn to them.

What makes these people different from the rest is NOT a "natural ability" or something they were born with. They possess no clear advantage over anyone else. The difference is that they've made a CHOICE to be this way. These people have DECIDED to live their life the way they want and have manifested rituals that make them the way they are.

You are what you repeatedly do and think every day. You are defined by your RITUALS—what you do on a consistent basis—and how you think. If you're always miserable, unhappy, anxious, living in fear, etc...it's because you have RITUALS that you may not even be aware of that are creating these emotions in your mind on a consistent basis. You've literally TRAINED yourself to be this way through practice and conditioning.

Can you change? YES. Can you be happy, confident, and passionate each day? YES.

How, you ask? DECIDE—it's that simple. You hold the power to your own destiny. You get to choose how each day unfolds and how you handle everything that may come your way.

When I was asked to participate in this book anthology, I took a hard look at what I manifest and bring about on a daily basis. Did I have any success rituals that I used on a daily basis? Could I add value to this book? Did I have important things to share? After some thinking, I realized the answer was YES to all these questions. What I realized more than anything else was that I also had negative rituals I was unaware of and they were sabotaging my plans for success! I began to examine very closely not only the success rituals I pratice but other behaviors I do every day that steer me off my powerful, energetic path.

Do I go through every day like the people I described earlier? Not nearly as often as I would like. I have, however, begun to take control of my thinking and my rituals.

The message and lesson of manifestation is so very important and yet so unknown to many of us still.

I do several things on a daily/weekly basis that have become my success rituals. Anyone who knows me knows I am the queen of "to-do" lists. So much so that if I do something and it wasn't on the list, I add it to the list just to cross it off. Yes, I am *that* person! Why deny myself the pleasure of crossing something off the list? There's just no better feeling than crossing items off your list—well, at least not until you cross the LAST item off your list! But then again, is there really ever a "last" item on the list? I think it's just a myth—there is just no such thing as a last item! At least not for the successful person, anyway! I poke fun at myself here but it is important to feel accomplished. That is what propels you to move ahead and do more to become more successful. So go ahead, add that missing item to the list and cross if off—don't deny yourself the pleasure of acting a little crazy!

One ritual I have is self-talk. I talk to myself about the day ahead of me, what I need to accomplish, and what I need to do to make it happen. Then I write it all down.

When I get in the car to head out for the day, I don't listen to the news—I only want positive things first thing in the morning. I can catch up on the news later in the day. I try to think of three things every morning that make me happy—and I mean, really happy. After I do this, it's pretty hard to get that smile off my face. Sometimes just fun music is what wakes me up and makes me happy. If I'm happy, I'm more creative and therefore more productive.

At the end of each day, you must ask yourself, are you proud of what you accomplished today? Did it add value to the successful path you have mapped out for yourself? That's one way to keep yourself on the straight and narrow.

Another ritual I am starting to do more and more every day is to read or listen to an audio from a top trainer in my field or in network marketing. The wealth of knowledge you can gain through this will be phenomenal and can propel you to the top of your field.

"Everything you can imagine is real." – Pablo Picasso

Some of you may be thinking, how do I even get started creating success rituals? How do I manifest the results I am looking for? The steps to successful manifestation *can* be achieved, but they require work, patience, faith, and trust to be put in on our behalf.

One way would be to create a vision board. It is probably one of the most valuable visualization tools available to you. It serves as your image of the future—a tangible representation of where you are going. It represents your dreams, your goals, and where you want to be in life.

It is a collage of images, pictures, and affirmations of your dreams and all of the things that make you happy. The saying "a picture is worth a thousand words" certainly applies to a vision board.

Vision boards are a great way to make you feel positive. Base it on something specific you wish to accomplish or obtain. Hang your vision board in a place you will see every day. View your board at least once a day, and focus on the objects, sayings, and theme of your board. Dreams change, you change, life changes. Don't be afraid to change your board to reflect more specific thoughts, or a new theme. Place a picture of yourself in the center as it shows you being surrounded by the things you desire. Posting the vision board in a place where you will see it every day is very powerful and keeps everything you desire alive within your consciousness, creating the attraction.

You can also create a "me" wall. This will have things like awards you have received or awards someone you mentored received. It should have all the things that show the success you have had and are having. Perhaps the first dollar you made in your business, and any other "firsts" you have experienced along the way in your career or business.

FINAL THOUGHTS

Just DECIDE. If you spend a lot of time thinking about your problems, they will grow bigger and you will give them more power over you. Focus on your dreams and your goals. Keep them in the forefront of your mind from the moment you wake up, all day, and until you go to bed at night. The great thing is that your thoughts are yours! They are completely under your control. So you might as well use them to benefit you. Whatever you think about long enough and intently enough will become a reality for you. That is because your thoughts direct your actions from moment to moment and day to day. Replaying the mental vision and image of where or who you would like to be is the key catalyst in swinging your vision from a mere daydream into reality! See yourself accomplishing your goals — imagine yourself succeeding in your dream. Begin to dress, talk, and look like the person you want to be. Say the things you would like to be said about you as if you have already achieved your goal.

I'm sure some of you are saying, *but I don't have time to do all these different things.* And to you I say this: successful people don't *have* time, they MAKE time! This reminds me of an old saying, "If you want something done, ask a busy person to do it."

Having a plan for each day of your life helps you to be PROACTIVE instead of REACTIVE. You aren't just reacting to the demands of others, but you're consciously designing and creating your day while moving in the direction towards your goals and dreams.

You are on display every day. Manifest the results you want. Show people what you want by your actions. Reveal your plans for success!

And just in case you are wondering…Yes, I do "manifest in high heels!"

MICHELLE BARR

Michelle Barr is a business coach for intuitive women. Michelle helps you translate your soul purpose into a tangible, step-by-step plan to create sacred success in your personal and business life. Michelle supports and guides you to move forward in all areas to create a life you love that supports and sustains you. Michelle has been a personal transformation specialist for over twenty years and loves to help people create what she calls "sacred success" by offering powerfully practical and spiritually-rich tools to help you create a better life and a better business now!

🏠 www.michellebarr.com.

FROM LIVING BY DEFAULT TO LIVING BY DESIGN

By Michelle Barr

Sometimes it amazes me what I have created here.

I mean, I really did it! After turning my life into an experiment for the law of attraction, I have completely shifted, from living by default into living by design.

I lived by default because I wasn't in control. Everyone else was. Others called the shots; I just followed along. My husband, parents, children, friends, and co-workers controlled my emotions. My job controlled my work hours and paychecks. I submitted myself to the demands and expectations of others without regard to the effects it would have on me.

Despite the circumstances, I figured living by default was the norm. It was how life was meant to be—miserable and unfulfilling. We can't all be happy all the time, I thought. And, believe me, there are plenty of people who will gather around you and support THAT belief.

When I came to that place in 2003 where I was sick of everything in my life, I couldn't believe it. I had been here before. The first time, I had taken control of myself and my life, gone through an intense spiritual awakening, and had created a whole new life. Yet, a decade and a half later, here I was again.

I've rebooted my life from miserable circumstances—including an unhappy marriage and draining career—TWICE. The second time, it stuck!

The first time, I was just intuitive and awakened enough to pull myself out of my miserable circumstances and create a better life. The problem was, I didn't know what I was doing. I wasn't *consciously* creating. So I ended up creating some of what I wanted and a lot of what I didn't.

It wasn't until I committed myself to learning how to consciously create life on my terms that I transformed my life for the better—with lasting results.

When all the buzz began about the law of attraction, and I woke up a second time, I knew they were saying something that felt right. It was like I was being reminded of something I already knew. But I, like many others, struggled to use the universal principles put forth to me to transform my life for the better.

Something inside me recognized I was standing at this place again, with some sort of do-over—a pop quiz from the Universe to do it differently the second time around. And this time, I finally learned how to master it.

I embarked on a journey that day I may not have agreed to if I had known where it would take me. But, from where I stand now, I would do it all over again.

If you are one of those people who feel that *The Secret* and the whole law of attraction movement failed them, I get it. *The Secret* served a purpose of bringing this ancient wisdom and universal thought into the mass consciousness, but, in order to do that, it had to be watered down.

People watched the movies, read the books, listened to the audios over and over, joined groups to help them make it work, carried rose quartz in their purse alongside their gratitude journal, updated daily with "five things I am grateful for today"…and, still, it wasn't working.

After several weeks, or even months of practice, many people failed to manifest what they most desired. They still didn't love their work. They still didn't have enough money. Their marriage was still on the rocks. Their spouse still threatened to leave. Their children refused to behave. Creditors and bill collectors continued to call.

Since they failed to get results, they figured the law of attraction was nothing more than feel-good "woo-woo, hocus pocus." It might work for some, but for the most part, they decided it was for suckers, and they discarded the beliefs they had been holding onto like a lifeline. They felt jilted and resigned themselves to living their life as is—by default.

Still, something about this whole law of attraction thing was ringing true to me. What did I have to lose? I was already dissatisfied with my life. I was pretty miserable. So, I made that decision in the heat of an inspired moment to turn my life into an experiment for the law of attraction. I could not have known it would completely transform not only my life but the life of my husband and children, and it would become not just my life but my life's work.

You see, the problem is not the law of attraction. The law of attraction works. In fact, it's infallible, and it's on…twenty-four hours a day, seven days a week, whether you believe in it or not. You just have to understand how to work with it.

The truth is, you can't get what you want by just *thinking* happy thoughts about it. You have to *take action*. That is the real secret. It's the key to everything.

After all that, this is going to seem so simple, possibly too simple, but here is how it works. To make it even easier for you, as you are learning something new and putting it into practice, I have broken it down into a simple exercise with four easy steps. Take out a blank index card for this.

1. Set an intention of something you want to create. Write it down on a notecard.

Be very clear. Be very specific. The important thing is to stay with what you want without regard to how it could happen. Leave the *how's* to the Universe. This is an important universal law that will absolutely determine your results.

2. Come up with new actions you are willing to take to make this happen. Write them down on the other side of the note card.

This is not about springing into action and just doing, doing, doing. This is about getting into a quiet, reflective place and connecting with what you want and writing it down. Then, become inspired and write down actions you are inspired to take.

Ask and it is given is a universal principle. It is found in every sacred text, and it is absolutely true. When you ask, the Universe always begins delivering to you what you are asking for. Most people just aren't prepared for how it actually shows up in comparison to how they expect it to show up. When you ask, begin immediately to watch for opportunities to show up. And remember this, they will not be logical, comfortable, or convenient. They will stretch and grow you. If you didn't need to grow and stretch to receive them, you would already have them.

3. Follow through with at least one.

Get into inspired, aligned action right away. Take one action, then watch for feedback. Stay in action. Learn to act, assess, and adjust. Course correct as needed. Just don't stop. The Universe will continue to give you feedback. Watch for breadcrumbs, and follow the breadcrumbs, even when—ESPECIALLY when—they don't make sense. Just follow the breadcrumbs.

4. Make it happen! And watch the Universe go to work for you.

The Universe responds to true need. It does not play the when/then game. You always have to take the first step. Then it will rush in to support you. You are building a trust muscle here. Try this first with small things—less important things. Don't try this right away with things that trigger you emotionally. The easiest things to manifest are those things you have high desire for and low resistance to.

Hang on to the card. Hang it up where you can see it. Track your progress on it. This works best when you can stay engaged but detached from the outcome. You can affirm and write on the card, "Thank you for this or something better." Leave the door open for something to show up that is better than what you are asking for. You can't even imagine the miracles the Universe can deliver to you! And when it shows up, express gratitude and tack the card up on your celebration board, or tuck it into your gratitude journal…then go for the next one.

The key here is these things at first are things you *do*. They are new ways of thinking, new patterns of behavior, new ways of doing things. And, over time, they become more than things you do—they become a way of living and a way of being.

Right before your eyes, your life will transform.

Living this way has allowed me to create a vision of the life I want to live and then create a business that supports and sustains that life—and it changes with me, grows with me, and evolves with me. It always supports me and my life first, and as I am supported, I am able to touch and impact many in the world.

KATRINA CAVANOUGH

For twenty-one years, Katrina Cavanough has worked with thousands of people as a grief and trauma therapist. She is now an inspirational speaker, life strategist, and spiritual change agent. Katrina has been featured successfully on major national TV, print, and radio media in Australia. Katrina is the author of *Wisdom for Your Life* and is also the author of the CD, *Happy Little Hearts – Health & Healing Meditations for Children*. Katrina is also the spirituality coach for Balance by Deborah Hutton.

🏠 **www.katrinacavanough.com**

🐦 **www.twitter.com/katcavanough777**

🅕 **www.facebook.com/katrinacavanough**

ℐs MANIFESTING MIRACLES DRIVING YOU CRAZY?

By Katrina Cavanough

Sometimes this manifestation process can feel like it's driving you crazy! Right? Even though I know I am a powerful creator of my own experience—with countless examples of just how reliable the laws of the universe are—at times, I have been known to find myself in a frustrated frenzy.

I know that whatever I focus upon I receive. The tricky part for me is that I am impatient. I want to know *when*, I want to know *why not now*, and sometimes I want to know *how*.

In fact, it's my own experience with frustration and impatience that has given me clarity. Once I realized this fabulous fact, I felt immediately liberated. And because I feel liberated, I want everyone to know so that they can be inspired to continue manifesting in their own lives. So here it is.

I now know that it is impossible to stop the laws of the universe from operating in our lives. We can feel impatience, fear, worry, and self-doubt, and it won't have any impact at all. Not one little bit!

I know this because I have achieved so many wonderful experiences, opportunities, better relationships, and material things—even when I have felt this way. Over and over again, as I felt frustrated, complained, and worried my day away, the universe just kept on delivering.

In my twenties, when my treating specialist advised me that I had Grave's disease and then laid out the list of unattractive treatment options, I found myself naturally thinking and really knowing deep within myself, "No, I do not have Grave's disease. I am healthy and will be free of this soon." I complied with the treatment that was supposed to stabilize my out-of-balance body, took the medication, and I sat months later in front of the doctor, where he advised I was most fortunate to have been cured. I would not need any further medical intervention. I was relieved but not surprised.

Again, in my late thirties, when a specialist physician told me that my second pregnancy would be the same as the first—and that meant insulin-dependent gestational diabetes—I looked this lovely, kind, and clever man in the eyes and said, "No, this will not happen to me. This time I will have a healthy pregnancy."

He gently replied, "Katrina, it is not a matter of *if*, it's just *when*." I smiled, reassured him that I would undertake the regular tests to monitor the situation, and as I passed each test, I felt such gratitude in my heart.

The list of other wonderful opportunities and experiences are endless, really. At the time of writing this list, I have manifested the right people around me to have my work pitched to global media platforms. I am a regular contributor to many international media outlets, such as MariaShriver.com. I am speaking now at international events.

For two years, I held a clear intention that I would have a national multimedia platform here in Australia to write, speak, and share my work. This wonderful opportunity unfolded into my life during an interview with Deborah Hutton about the release of my book, *Wisdom for Your Life* (Allen & Unwin). During the interview, Deborah Hutton's producer invited me to join the Balance By Deborah Hutton (www.balancebydeborahhutton.com.au) team as their intuition and spirituality coach. And there it was—easily unfolding in my life once again.

I have also realized a serious dream to be a published author with a national publishing company. I have a book contract with Allen &

Unwin, who published *Wisdom for Your Life*—what I have learned from those who passed over. *Wisdom for Your Life* is now available in Australia, New Zealand, USA, and Canada. I have also published a CD with Blue Angel Publishing—*Happy Little Hearts – Health &Healing Meditations for Children*—now available worldwide.

In 2011, I set the intention that by the end of that year, I would have a national media profile. Never in a million years could I have comprehended what followed. I was selected out of hundreds of people to be one of Australia's top 10 psychics to be featured on a prime time TV show on one of the major networks here in Australia. This meant I was able to experience significant national media coverage, including national TV, online media, radio, and national magazines. And this has continued onward over the years as my book and CD were released.

My greatest blessings are my two happy and healthy daughters, Phoebe and Kate, and my loving husband, Alan—who is a constant support and a wonderful father to our two girls.

The list goes on and includes countless jobs with the right conditions, establishing my own successful business doing the work I love.

The key here is that I have experienced all of these achievements and miracles even though, on a regular basis, I would sometimes find myself quite upset as my feelings of impatience and frustration would nearly overwhelm me.

As experiences, success, and material things just rolled into my life over and over again, I had to accept the fact that I can worry all I want, but once I set my intentions, took consistent action steps, and believed that all things are possible, then nothing—including my little doubtful mind—could impede the process.

Whenever I talk with people at my workshops and in coaching sessions about creating the life they want, there is always one sticking point. People always worry about the impact of their own self-doubt and worry. This appears to be one of the greatest myths about the process of creating—that you can in some way impact this great flow of energy with your own fears.

Over and over again I am asked the same question. "What if I worry, or have doubts about whether the 'process' will work? Does that get in the way or slow down the creation process?"

Each person usually then describes the way they use the laws of the universe to create the life they want. They always start out strong, focused, and fueled by an emotional high. They set their intentions and begin to take daily action, moving toward the essence of that which they are creating. This is a great start.

Then as time goes by, the natural human response is to begin to doubt the process and themselves. It's usually at this point fear creeps in and my clients tell me they find themselves full of worry about whether their self-doubt is "ruining the process." Right about at this, point most people slow down or even stop taking the daily action steps toward their intentions, and this is where we see people give up.

I invite you, right now, to consider that your self-doubt, impatience, and worry do not impact "the flow" in any way whatsoever. If you accept this understanding then you have taken yourself off the hook. Phew! This means you are allowed to be human and have regular and normal responses of frustration and worry. So feel free to impatiently ask, "When, oh when, is it showing up in my life?"

The truth though is that whilst self-doubt does not in any way affect the creation process, it does impact the way you experience your everyday life. It can take away the joy. And for this reason alone, I am working on that one. I am keen to fine-tune this aspect of my perception so I can feel calm as I experience the unfolding. It's a wonderful work in progress. And I am happy to share the journey with you. In the meantime, create away and remember that self-doubt is OK.

JESSICA McCLESKEY HOOD

Jessica is a women's weight loss expert who has radically cracked the code on losing weight permanently. After struggling with body image issues for two-thirds of her life, she created her own weight-loss system, lost fifty pounds, and has kept it off for years! She has dedicated her career to helping empower women to learn a gentle, feminine, and permanent solution to weight loss that not only shrinks their bodies but expands their lives, sensuality, and dreams. In her thriving practice, she shows sophisticated, lovely women struggling to lose fifteen pounds or more how to experience extraordinary results that she, too, has lived.

🏠 www.sensualweightloss.com

📷 www.instagram.com/jhmccleskey

f www.facebook.com/jessica.m.hood.1

🐦 www.twitter.com/JHMcCleskey

MANIFESTATION 17

Sensually Manifest Your Svelte, Empowered, Goddess Self

By Jessica McCleskey Hood

What I see missing in this art of contorting our bodies and losing weight most is the divine—the WHY. The subconscious root of the desire to feel svelte and sexy is not to match that of magazines, Facebook postings, Instagram shots, and Hollywood-types alike—the subconscious root is to *embody the goddess*. The universal language of beauty is love. When a woman radiates love and abundance, — the only thing that really exists—, she radiates beauty from aligning with her truth. And that is sensual, empowering, and sexy.

Personally and frenziedly, I have traipsed across each of the far ends of the spectrum with my body. I have been too thin, dabbling exhaustedly in Adderall prescriptions, bulimia, anorexia, diets, pills, guilt, vanity-sizing, one-on-one nutritional support, extreme exercise, cleanses, creams, laxatives, powdered drinks, and sugar-, carb-, and fat-free fare. I have also unabashedly pushed the edges of obesity with emotional eating, binge eating, sugar and coffee addiction, depression, sloth-lifestyle, lackluster jobs, non-existent exercise, emotionally abusive relationships, and paralytic belief systems. I was constantly living in fear and lack, which was reflected in my body—all in the name of maintaining thinness, striving to be thin, or wallowing in self-pity that I wasn't *thin enough,* because being thin was the shiny, idolized prize. If I were thin, then the world was mine for the taking. These habits were used as numbing agents and a giving away of power. My weight antics left me destitute of the goddess energy that resides within every woman.

In Sensual Weight Loss, I teach women to fearlessly connect to their divinity. When women honor passions and deep desires by way of sensual intuition, everything else, including their natural weight, falls into place. Women bridge the gap between their conscious and subconscious weight loss desires while adoring the trail they blaze. By choosing to give every moment meaning, you become so in love and intoxicatingly mesmerized by the minute-to-minute magic of life that your fixation on weight loss dissipates. Life feels oh-so fulfilling. You become a vessel for big, holy love. Then one day, you look in the mirror and your figure has shifted. Love pours out of your eyes, as everything around you has transformed with your commitment to love and abundance as the journey's standard. It is reflected EVERYWHERE. The fear of gaining the weight back is non-existent. Radiating your light and giving joy back to the planet becomes your prime focus, all because you have filled your cup first with a hefty dose of L&A.

It takes patience to live in a place of sensual intuition—magical, unwavering trust. There is no promise of a "Four Weeks to a Twenty-Pound, Lighter You" plan here. (Yet, that no longer matters.) A lady like yourself has to "brave it up" and follow your internal drumming. You embrace feeling a little crazy along your way. And there is something extremely hot about looking your kinks in the eyes and making love to them. There is a confidence that emerges from graciously bowing down to your edgier expressions and nurturing them in lieu of a brutal shunning, which rouses and fans your sensual empowerment. These are seen as a woman's greatest seducers and teachers. What is going on below the surface? How can you learn to love your current state and "disreputable" habits so much so they fade away and change into something more stunning than you could have ever imagined? You must declare and salute the wildfire within.

The path to greeting your divine goddess is honoring your sensual intuition. Meaning you must let go of old-school logic. No more counting calories, weighing yourself, or following protocols. You *feel* your way there. How brave. You become your grandest listener and lover. It is a rewiring of motivation. No longer is the external motivator of "body perfection" the impetus for your physical transformation. You use your internal desire to be a messenger of love, abundance, and peace as your siren. A love and abundance mindset becomes your home base over a number on a scale or dress size.

When a woman is holding onto extra weight, emotionally eating, and despising her body, it is a reflection that she is dishonoring a part of her sacred makeup. She is out of alignment with her goddess. She has bestowed her power to a habit, belief, relationship, career, or experience that does not serve her best and highest good. However, and this may sting, she is *choosing* to do so. She cuffed herself in chains, and there is nothing wrong with that. To acknowledge this is bold. Many women unconsciously cushion themselves because it falsely feels safer than acknowledging their power-zapping reality. Sensual Weight Loss is not for the faint-hearted. It is for women ready to say, "Yes! This is my life! I am responsible for every experience I have had, am having, and will have. And it is all happening for me. There are parts I would like to shift. Anything is possible. I am a co-creator of my reality. To create a life I love, I choose empowerment in all scenarios. Through an empowered mindset, my body finds alignment. I am thrilled about this journey. I am the only one who can give myself permission to go there, yet I never tread alone. No diet will lead me to lasting empowerment, but my sensuality will."

So, I have a couple of tools for you. I like to address weight loss from a scope of angles to keep a steady composition of head in the clouds, toes on the earth, and heart in service of self and society. Such is the sensually intuitive way of the empowered goddess.

GUIDE ONE:

Accessing your goddess: food, movement, nature, laughter, inspiration, rest, orgasms. There are many ways to access your lady of light.

Food. Eat high-vibrational, whole foods that create alkalinity, reduce inflammation, harness focus, relinquish emotional seesaws, and make you feel beautiful! For many, this is a food style of raw or vegan fare with a touch of clean and humanely-sourced, happy animal protein upon your body's request. Think whole foods: fruits, vegetables, superfoods, whole-food healthy fats, and cacao! Let go of processed foods.

Move. Move your body daily, as she is your temple and enjoys being expressed—but love your expression. No rigid routines.

Nature. Be in the energy of the earth. Kneel on it. Walk barefoot. Speak to it.

Laughter. Upon hitting an internal place of discomfort, turn to laughter, inspiration, and rest.

Orgasms. Have them and have them often. Pleasure yourself and see it as sacred. It is one of the most promising ways to access sensual intuition and weight release. Orgasms and receiving go in tandem, and in order to receive them, you must let go.

GUIDE TWO:

<u>Lady Moon:</u> You are connected to the moon. Your sex drive and weight will fluctuate every month with her waxing and waning, but if you love the changes instead of demonizing them, you will reap the full benefits of every occasion. Each phase is equally gorgeous and laced with intuitive gifts. You can bow to her and hand her your woes and thank her for your celebrations. She will always encourage you to dream and tap into your intuition. Use her. Converse with her. See her as an internal and external home for your own divine goddess. You will begin to see the splendor of the birth, dying, and rebirth cycles in everything, including your cravings and body shape. Your understanding of your cyclical nature will feel empowering! You will begin to hone in on a deeper connection to what you really need—and fearlessly allow it in.

GUIDE THREE:

<u>Goddesshood:</u> Encircle yourself with women who lift you up and love you unconditionally, yet mirror you when you are stepping back into fear and lack. Those women who live fearlessly. Those women who are conscious of their words, their bodies, and our planet. The women who

know how to receive and give, equally. And if they are not already in your life, ask for them to appear (from a place of love and abundance, of course). Surround yourself with awakened goddesses.

GUIDE FOUR:

<u>Love and abundance over fear and lack:</u> The most empowering mindset to FEEL your sensuality is love and abundance. Commonly, society is prone to amplifying fear and lack. Everywhere. People use it as a defense mechanism for not stepping into their power. Lack leads to fear, fear feeds into guilt. Guilt and fear are perfect collaborators for the creation of emotional eating, body hate, and weight gain. Surround yourself with what makes you feel good. How long you hold onto the people, places, beliefs, or experiences that portray lack and fear typically dictates how long you hold on to the weight. Take the leap. Release the fear, release the weight. Love and abundance are your birthrights. Live in this place and you cannot fail to live in alignment with your sensually, intuitive, svelte, and empowered goddess.

TRYPHENNA C. BASTIAN

Tryphenna Bastian is a widowed mother of five children. She was born and raised in Decatur, GA, and now resides in Lithonia, GA. In addition to writing, she enjoys acting, dancing, and spending time with her family. She worked in the technology industry for almost seventeen years and is now pursuing her entrepreneurial dream. She is a full-time student at SUNY Empire State College in Saratoga Springs, NY, in pursuit of her bachelor's degree in business. She is an active member of Berean Christian Church and loves to volunteer in the community.

🏠 tryphennacbastian.legalshieldassociate.com

✉ tryphennacbastian@legalshieldassociate.com

f www.facebook.com/tryphenna/

🐦 www.twitter.com/Trypout

in www.linkedin.com/pub/tryphenna-jackson-bastian/4/583/134/

📷 www.instagram.com/trypout76

MANIFESTATION 18

$\mathcal{T}$HE SECRET WITHIN US

By Tryphenna C. Bastian

The Bible shows in Luke 8:17, "For nothing is secret, that shall not be made manifest; neither anything hid, that shall not be known and come abroad." Nothing is secret to us. Everything we need is right within our grasp. The most popular types of books now are all about *100 Simple Secrets of Great Relationships*, *The Secret to Success*, *The Secret*—but to be honest, I don't believe any of the information we need for greatness is much of a secret. The only secret is to unlock what is inside of you and work with the tools with which you were born. Each of us came to our life assignments knowing what is needed to accomplish our purpose. What causes us to lose our paths? Why do we struggle to see the manifestation of the promises? Only one thing causes a barrier to our blessings. The key to manifesting is to remove all fear.

Whatever we concentrate on is what we allow to manifest in our lives. Throughout my life, I have seen this practice at work. The early years of my life were very difficult. I grew up in very challenging circumstances, rife with poverty and dysfunction. I was an intelligent girl full of promise, but I did not have the right support team to show me how to train my thoughts to obtain a better life. As a result, I became very bitter and resentful. Why was I not like the other children? Why were they able to succeed at higher levels? I was succeeding too, but even I knew it was way below my potential. I was very angry. I blamed everyone: my parents, my siblings, God, my classmates, my church, and my community. As a result, I became an adult who was only able to manifest disappointment and hatred. I was disappointed with how my life had developed. People would always say, "When life gives you lemons, make lemonade." All I could see was that I did not have a pitcher, sugar, or water. I knew I was continuing the cycle of poverty and not doing anything close to the potential with which I was blessed. I was so disappointed I literally hated myself, and I hated everything around me. The hatred manifested into physical health problems and journeys into experimentation with drugs and alcohol. This hatred also caused such a low self-esteem that I surrounded myself with very unhealthy relationships. I bounced from relationship to relationship, grabbing all the negative portions, taking them with me and transferring them to the next one. It showed in my work as well. I was a mess.

When you have finally reached a breaking point, you will be forced to change. I was at my breaking point. I had begun to hear rumors about myself at work. "She'll never be promoted because she's too negative." "Her work is good but her attitude is the problem." "Why doesn't she ever smile?" In the past, I laughed when I heard these rumors. I easily brushed them off by saying, "These people do not know me. If they only knew what I have been through, they would wonder why I still allow myself to breathe." Then, one day, everything began to change. A new manager was assigned to my department. In our first meeting together, she told me something I had never heard—"Do not allow anyone to control who you will be today. You, and only you, control your actions and reactions." I was floored. All I knew was how to be the victim and blame everyone for everything that had ever happened to me. I cried in this meeting because I realized how ugly a person I had become. The inside of me must have looked like a war zone with casualties—like love, joy, and peace—just blown apart and scattered. I began to make the hard transition to become the person I knew I could be.

Fear creates obstacles, which impairs your vision. The hatred and disappointment had created such a fear in me that I could not see my way. The path was right in front of me, but it was like a heavy fog hung over it. I was walking in the right direction with the right guidance, but the clouds were too heavy. God has a way that will jolt you awake though. Every trial in this life can be that shock if we are ready. At this point, while I was fighting with my inner demons, life threw me for a loop. I was twenty-four years old and excited about my upcoming birthday—only five months away.

I had been struggling with sudden weight loss and problems with my vision so I decided to see a doctor. After many tests, the doctor was concerned and referred me to a specialist. A month of testing went by, and I was diagnosed with a brain tumor. I was in shock. I was finally at a point where I was ready to start making some changes and then I received this news. I was headed to my usual "Why me?" path, but then something hit me. If all these negative thoughts landed me at this place in my life, where would I go if I stayed on the path of positivity? I started looking at my life and what needed to be eliminated. I began to really seek the things that had been missing from my life for so long. Where I lacked love, I gave love. Where I lacked joy, I sought out joy. Where I lacked peace, I became peace. The areas of my life where I was not receiving these things were eliminated immediately. I ended a long-lasting relationship that I knew no longer had a place in my life. My attitude received a major adjustment. I began to read and absorb anything that was positive. I read my Bible more and took advantage of courses at work to enlighten me.

I was prescribed radiation surgery where I had a procedure that went into my brain to decrease the tumor. A requirement of the surgery was to be alert during the procedure, so I was able to watch television and nap. While in this state, I was really able to sit still and hear what life was saying. The doctor had told me if they had not operated sooner, I would have lost my sight due to the placement of the tumor on my optical nerve. As the doctors were removing the blockage so I could continue to see clearly, I realized I needed to continue to remove the blockages in my life so I could see more clearly. Once my vision was clear, then my purpose would be defined. At that moment, I made a decision to leave all the negativity behind and just learn to take life as it comes. I was never the same. The feedback was immediate. I began to hear new rumors. "I love being around her energy." "She's our shining star." "I want her on our project because it will be successful." I was amazed at how just changing my mindset could change my life so much.

As a result of learning to manifest the light that shines inside of me, I was able to begin to see a lot of awesome things come into my life. Love manifested into my life in the result of an awesome husband and family. Joy manifested by showing me that obstacles will come to us all, but how we relate and react to them is how success is measured. Peace manifested through learning to obtain my answers in the stillness by eliminating the clutter in my mind. I was finally able to grasp all the things for which I sought. The lesson to us all is that we will deal with adversities. No one in this earth escapes that part of the journey. We must understand that the light is in all of us, and until we let go of the fear and embrace the light, nothing will ever change. Everything will remain dark, depressed, and dismayed. Our perception is what makes the difference. Is this situation happening to us or for us? When it happens to us, we become the victims. When it happens for us, we become the conquerors.

to dismiss another option. Of course, this car analogy can be applied to anything and everything you are trying to attract.

The Universe knows what's best for you. It is *your job* to surrender. You can't see a picture as large as the eyes of the Universe. Trust you will get exactly what you need. Try not to feel disappointed when things don't go or come your way. Offset this by getting busy with the next doing part. Keep going, keep shopping, and keep researching. Sooner or later, you will reach a wonderful result. Most people quit a second before they achieve. I have seen so many people leave college a week before they graduate. Stamina is a soul quality that will serve you well. Increase your stamina by driving yourself toward your desire. Every time you feel like giving up or throwing in the towel, tell yourself this: "If I do quit and allow myself to be defeated, what will happen then? Where do I go from there? Is that the destination I desire?" I can assure you the answer will be no. Take one more step, that's all it takes—one more step toward your goal. When you push through the fears, doubts, and obstacles in your way, that's when the Universe takes your hand and lifts you onto the magic carpet that is destined for your greatest desires.

JESSICA GRAVES

Jessica is a wife, mom, book-lover, and freelancer/business owner. She has always been drawn to live a creative life, particularly as a writer. As an outlet and direction for her creativity, she started a blog where she works to refocus her efforts to live creatively.

After leaving a corporate job, she started Graves Writing & Publishing, Inc., to provide teams with high quality documentation, desktop publishing, and project management services.

Jessica is also a book coordinator for Coaching & Success, which allows her to combine her passion for books, writing, and helping others.

 www.linkedin.com/in/jessicaagraves

 www.graveswriting-publishing.com

 creativerecentering.wordpress.com

 www.facebook.com/Jessica.Graves.29

MANIFESTATION 20

𝒯HE DIRECTION OF MY DREAMS: FAITH, OPTIMISM, AND INTENTION

By Jessica Graves

I read in Anne Lamott's *Bird by Bird* that "a person's faults are largely what make him or her likable." In the hope that this is true, I want to confess that I don't have it all together. Enumerating my faults is more time and space than I have with you, but I don't want to give the impression that I am not also struggling with manifesting my goals. I've had some valuable breakthroughs, though. I've been lucky, and for the most part, I've had a good life. I attribute that the ways my goals have manifested through a combination of faith, optimism, and steadily moving with intention in the direction of my dreams.

One goal I had for as long as I can remember was to be a stay-at-home mom. My mom stayed home with my brother, sister, and me, and I always knew that when I became a mom, I wanted to do the same.

I began working toward and thinking about this goal long before I even became a mom. I opted to wait on graduate school because of plans to stay home with my kids (this proved to be a solid choice for me, especially due to a career change a few years after graduating from college). After I got a job, my husband and I waited to start a family until after he finished medical school. Knowing I wanted to stay home, we wanted to position our family for this in the future, and starting a family while I was the sole earner would not have aided my goal.

After deciding the time was right, it was not as easy to get pregnant as I'd expected. My mom always joked that all she had to do was think about getting pregnant and she was. I expected my experience to be the same—after all, I'd always taken after my mom in so many other ways. Unfortunately for me, that was not the case when it came to pregnancy. I managed to remain optimistic through the process though by reminding myself each month that it wasn't meant to be. In order for me to get the baby God intended for me, I had to be patient. My patience paid off when I was blessed with my beautiful boy.

During my pregnancy, I took steps to ensure I would be at home with my son as much as possible. I'd modified my dream slightly when I realized that I still needed something for *me* in addition to being a mom. I still wanted to work, but I wanted to cut back. I spoke with both my boss and HR. I drew up a plan for my modified work arrangement, and after some negotiating, we agreed on a shortened work week and some days working from home. I was thrilled with the new arrangement because it meant more time with my baby, but at the same time, I was still working over thirty hours a week—which was far from the stay-at-home-mom dream I'd been harboring.

When my son was eight months old, major layoffs occurred at my company. And while I had never feared for my job before, after a project I was working on got cut, my name was added to the layoff list. Suddenly, I was dealing with the rejection of a layoff, the sadness of losing a job I enjoyed with people I liked working with, and the fear of what would come next. In my mind, I just lost the closest thing I had to being at home with my son. I worried that I wouldn't be able to find another job with reduced hours.

Luckily, I wasn't forced into making a decision immediately and I was able to take some time to ponder what my next move would be. I was also blessed by my former company with the support of a job counselor to help me decide my next move. As I studied my options, I began to realize that working as a consultant and freelancer may lead to exactly the kind of hours and control I wanted. I slowly began to realize that losing my job was one of the best things that could have happened to me. It was a job I enjoyed, and I had amazing benefits, and for those reasons, it would have been nearly impossible for me to leave on my own. I began to see that the Universe was steering me toward my long-time goal of being a stay-at-home mom. The longer I was able to stay home during this search, the more convinced I was it was the right move for me.

I also realized that I was still missing something as an individual. As much as I loved being a wife and mom and having the opportunity to spend tons of quality time with my son while running our household, I needed a fulfilling venture that was for *me*. As I began reaching this point, I received an email from a former colleague offering me work as a consultant. Again, it seemed that God—or the universe, or whatever your preferred term is—was guiding me toward my goal by offering just the opportunity I needed. This offer was the first step toward starting Graves Writing & Publishing, Inc.—my place to focus on providing high quality writing and desktop publishing services to my clients.

One of my favorite parts of work was always interacting with people. Working from home as a writer was not aiding too much in that department. As I decided to expand my menu to provide project management services, it started me on the hunt for new opportunities. And again the universe blessed me when I found Christine Marmoy at Coaching & Success. As a lifelong bibliophile and aspiring writer looking for work in project management, could a more perfect job present itself than as a book coordinator for a publisher, working with authors to make their own goals a reality? Books, writing, helping people—some of my biggest passions all checked off—and I would still be working on my own schedule at home, which was completely conducive to being the stay-at-home mom of my dreams.

The final chapter I have to share of my still-changing story is happening right now as I sit here writing. I've always had aspirations of being a writer. I started a blog that I'm not very good at updating (remember when I said I'm still a work in progress?!). I try to write when I can carve out some time, but I'm still working on making it a priority. But again, God and Christine helped me along when I was offered a spot in this book. As I sit here writing, my son sits across the table, pen in hand, and we write together.

Pablo Picasso said, "Inspiration exists, but it has to find you working." That rings so true for me as I look back at all of the ways my goals were manifested. When I chose optimism in the face of a bad situation and trusted in my faith that all things happen for a reason, I was repeatedly blessed with promising opportunities. But it was by always working toward my goals that I was able to take those opportunities and make something out of them. I came across this quote from one of my favorite authors, Elizabeth Gilbert, and while in the context of her quote she is speaking of religion, I think her advice can easily be applied to manifesting your goals: "You take whatever works from wherever you can find it, and you keep moving toward the light."

CELESTE JOHNSON

At forty-three years young, Celeste Johnson is a vivacious woman with a passion for travel who knows what it's like to manifest her dreams into reality. Having received her bachelor's degree in international business, she is currently a project manager for CM Publishing and has found herself inspired to become an author, as she has recently returned to the United States to fulfill her dream of opening a non-profit organization for military veterans. With her pup, Loki, in tow, Celeste is ready to manifest her destiny in high heels.

✉ celeste@coachingandsuccess.com

✉ whisperingmeadowssantuary@gmail.com

in www.linkedin.com/in/celestejohnson2

MANIFESTATION 21

ℛETURNING TO FAITH

By Celeste Johnson

"Create the highest, grandest vision possible for your life, because you become what you believe."
— Oprah Winfrey

Have you ever wondered how you ended up in a certain situation? Well, that was me about a year ago, right around the same time my job finished. I had a lot of free time while looking for another job and found myself questioning every decision I ever made leading up to that very moment. Wondering how different my life would have turned out had I taken a different road.

In order for you to understand how I got to the position I am now, I need to take you back seventeen years ago. When I decided I wanted something, I would spring into action and act as if it had already happened—and then it would happen. For example, when I was going to college, I asked my dad if I could get a tattoo. He told me I could once I graduated (assuming I would forget by then), so I decided to graduate in three years instead of four and booked the appointment to get my tattoo the day after my graduation. You know what? I did graduate in three years and got my tattoo the day after I graduated.

I never doubted any decision I ever made. OK, sometimes the decisions weren't necessarily the right ones but I never regretted making the decision. I just took the leap of faith, constantly. After I graduated, I set the intention of going to England. I never stopped talking about England—to the point where everyone was just sick and tired of hearing about it. I finally found a job as internal sales rep with an IT networking company. Guess what happened six months into the job? An opportunity presented itself to go and work in their European headquarters in England! As you can imagine, I jumped at the opportunity.

I arrived in England in March 1997, and I can tell you that was a huge adventure for me, along with experiencing a lot of firsts. Moving away from my parents where I was more than an hour's drive and living abroad in a new country was a lot to get used to, but I managed to embrace the experience with lots of enthusiasm and eyes wide open.

After four months of living in England, I met someone. Three months later, we moved into together—that was another first for me...living with a man. Living with someone else is a really big learning curve, and I realized I may not have been ready for all the responsibility that came with it, such as communicating, sharing, and the rest. Being an only child meant never having to share with siblings. Don't get me wrong, I shared all my toys with my friends, but it's not the same as sharing with someone you live with.

As the years went on, I began to doubt every decision I ever made. I'm not kidding. It was just ridiculous having to pull out the blank piece of paper and write out the pros and cons of everything to ensure I was making the right decision—and even then I wasn't sure I got it right. Looking back now, it seems so silly I didn't have enough faith in the Universe to guide me in the right direction, when unwavering faith is exactly how I got to England. Needless to say, anything that could go wrong did go wrong—in every aspect of my life. It's not surprising when you are trying to deal with everything on your own instead of putting it into the hands of the Universe.

Back to where I was a year ago...I am not kidding when I say I cried a lot about past mistakes, decisions I regretted making, not doing my part in my relationship (I could have done a lot more), not staying in touch with people that supported me—the list goes on and on. Then a lovely lady I met suggested a book to me called, *Way of the Peaceful Warrior* by Dan Millman, and one of things it talks about in the book is letting it flow and letting it go. I must admit it's something that is a bit of a struggle, but I have to keep reminding myself I cannot control what other people do but I can control how I react to any given situation. It's still a work in progress, but every day I get better at recognizing what I can't control.

I decided I had enough of things constantly falling apart and not working how I would have liked. I went back to having conversations with the Universe and asked for guidance on finding the right job for me by divine right. A couple of months later, I was contacted by Christine Marmoy about a position in her company, which of course was the right job for me—I am not joking when I say my life turned a corner. I can definitely say I am lucky enough to love my job and have a great boss who happily mentors me when I really need it. I get to work with some amazing people who have taught me so much and are still teaching me how to grow as a person.

For a long time, I had been toying with the idea of moving back to the US. Although opportunities came up, the timing was always wrong. But at the beginning of this year, I decided it was time for me to move home so I could be closer to my friends and family. I set the intention to move back on December 1, and then I set about coming up with my plan of action. I started working on tasks every day that would bring me closer to my goal. In July, I received a message from an amazing person who asked me why I was waiting until December to go home. I came up with all sorts of reasons, but in reality none of it made sense. This person offered to pay for my plane ticket to Boston. I ended up flying back to the US with my dog in August—instead of December. I will be forever grateful for that beautiful gesture.

I am getting myself back to some form of normality. I decided to take some very good advice to start my days with positive action. My days now begin like this:

- Workout

- Walk with the dog

- Meditate

- Read

I think it's supposed to be a power hour, but I expanded it to two hours so I can take my time and not feel rushed. I haven't been doing it for very long, but so far I'm feeling great and getting my productive groove on. In the evenings, I read some more and sometimes meditate again.

Below are the things I do to manifest what I want:

- List out my goals
- Set my intention(s)
- Take action to show the Universe I want what I'm asking for (digging those ditches)
- Have faith that it will happen
- Develop an attitude of gratitude—in fact, I started a gratitude journal and I list out ten things I'm grateful for everyday
- Act as if it has already happened
- Love the process

So you see, anyone—and I mean anyone—can manifest their dreams. If I can do it, so can you. Just take that first step and the Universe will guide. I'm still a work in progress, but soon I will be the phoenix rising from the ashes.

"The biggest adventure you can take is to live the life of your dreams."
– Oprah Winfrey

ERICA GORDON

Erica Gordon is certified professional coach specializing in helping moms follow their dreams without feeling guilty. She's a #1 international best-selling author, speaker, radio show host, CEO of Defining Success, LLC, and founder of Moms with DREAMS—a community for ambitious moms.

After recovering from a devastating divorce, Erica discovered her mission to empower moms everywhere. Erica spreads her message of empowerment through coaching and workshops, where she teaches moms, in all stages of motherhood, the importance of putting themselves first; shows them how to reconnect with themselves and their dreams; and supports them in their journey of creating the life they desire.

Erica lives in New Jersey with her four beautiful children and charming boyfriend.

- www.momswithdreams.com
- Erica@momswithdreams.com
- momsndreams@gmail.com
- www.facebook.com/momswithdreams
- www.twitter.com/momswithdreams

MANIFESTATION 22

You CAN CREATE THE LIFE YOU WANT

By Erica Gordon

I became a mom at the tender age of seventeen. Most of my family and teachers were upset and disappointed because I was a "shining star" — the one who was going to receive academic scholarships and become the first college graduate and attorney in our family. While everyone else was busy feeling sorry for me and trying to deal with the reality of me becoming a teen mom, I was busy planning my future. I made a promise to my dad that I would graduate high school on time and still earn my college degree. I was committed to succeed in life and do all the things I planned to do before I got pregnant.

I had always been driven, and I knew that I was more than just another statistic. I didn't allow my situation to cloud my vision. Even back then, I knew I would grow up and do something great with my life. At that time, I also knew that one day I wanted to mentor teenage moms and encourage them never to give up on their dreams. I graduated in the top 10 percent and walked with my high school class. My seven-month-old son was in the audience in his stroller, with my parents and sisters. After graduating, I relocated to Savannah, GA, with my son and his father and started college in January of the following year.

Ever since I was a little girl, I dreamed of having a loving husband and children. At twenty-two, I fell in love with a man who seemed perfect in every way. We got married very quickly and had three children together. After fourteen years, my marriage ended very painfully. I was devastated. For years I dealt with lies and infidelity, so I knew it was the best thing that could have happened to me, although it didn't feel that way at the time.

During my marriage, and in the process of raising four young children, I refused to give up on my dreams. I also refused to break the promise I made to my dad about earning a college degree. While the kids were young, I earned a certificate in residential design. I continued taking college courses here and there and eventually completed my BS in small business management and entrepreneurship.

After my ex-husband and I separated, I spent many days lying in bed, paralyzed with fear and pain, crying incessantly. I had many conversations with God, trying to figure out how I would put my life back together. I vividly remember one conversation in which I prayed and asked Him to deliver me from that pit of fear, loneliness, and pain. I promised God that if He got me out of that place, I would use my painful experience to help women who were going through a life-changing experience without support or guidance. It was during this time I discovered my calling in life — to empower women.

I mustered up a lot of strength and refocused on my dreams. I went back to school, earned my graduate degree, and became a certified professional coach. It was no walk in the park on any level. I was dealing with my emotional pain and baggage. I was learning how to navigate through life as a single mom with four kids, all while working a demanding full-time job. But I refused to allow my current situation to distract me from my grand vision and my life's calling.

Over the years, I have mastered the art of raising children, running a household, working full time, and achieving my dreams. People are amazed and often ask me how I do it. I used to tell them I didn't know, but now I am very clear now on how I do it all. God, my source and guiding light, has blessed me with all I need to create the life of my dreams.

In the middle of my divorce, I started my empowerment organization, Defining Success, LLC. I am an international best-selling author and compiler of *Motherhood Dreams & Success: You Can Have It All*. I am the CEO of Empower Me! Radio network and I host my weekly show on BoldRadioStation.com. My network and radio show are all about empowering women to create the life they desire in spite of their current circumstances or past experiences. I am the founder of the Moms With Dreams Community™ and Moms With Dreams University™. All of these accomplishments have taken place in the last eighteen months.

Sometimes it's hard for me to believe how far I've come in such a short amount of time. Less than two years ago, the life I have today was a distant dream—something I could see very faintly in the distance but didn't fully believe could be mine. Had I not been a woman of faith, with courage and strength, my story would be much different. Plenty of women give up on their dreams because life gets in the way. But that's not how you win. You win when your desire to succeed is bigger than any obstacle that gets in your way.

A few months ago, my faith was tested when my dad passed away. He was only sixty-one and mysteriously contracted a very rare bacterial infection—another devastating experience, to say the least. We were best friends. He was my biggest supporter. My dad's passing happened right at the beginning of a huge project—compiling my first anthology with women from across the world. This was another big dream of mine, but I didn't think I could make it happen given the circumstances.

I lost my dad and I was in mourning. I wanted to quit. I was overwhelmed with sadness. I began to pray even more than I did before. One day, I heard God's soft whisper, encouraging me to keep going. I looked for signs from my dad to tell me I could do it. I prayed for the strength to keep going and God granted it to me. I completed that project and my book became a best seller in five hours.

I could have used my father's passing as an excuse to throw in the towel. Instead, I used that experience as motivation to keep moving forward. I knew that he wouldn't have wanted me to give up on my dream because of him.

I learned how to create order in the midst of chaos. In order to achieve my dreams, I had to develop a high-level focus on the things that would help me get closer to them. There were specific steps I took to help me get where I am today.

Anyone can apply these steps to manifest their dreams:

1. Get crystal clear on your dreams and the vision you have for your life. You have to know where you want to go in order to get there.

2. Make self-care a top priority. No matter how badly you want something to happen, if you're not feeling well, you won't have the energy you need to put in the work.

3. Get connected with like-minded people who support you and your dreams. Build a community if you don't have this already. Support is critical to your success.

4. Create structure and implement systems that simplify your life. The road to success isn't easy, so whatever you can do to lessen your load will help.

5. Don't make excuses. Life will always be there and obstacles will show up. It's up to you to find the strength you need to keep going.

Society has a way of making women feel like it isn't natural for them to pursue goals and dreams after they have children. Often, women feel guilty and selfish because they are choosing something for themselves over their family. I beg to differ, and I know that isn't true. Your dreams are your dreams, and they were given to you for a reason. I am living proof that you can have it all despite your circumstances.

As long as you know what you want and are willing to do what it takes, you too can turn your dreams into your reality. Don't put your dreams off another day. Now is your time to claim the abundance that is just for you.

ADRIENNE S. SANTANA

Adrienne and her husband share three wonderful children and two grandchildren. Adrienne gives all credit and honor to God for the life he has gifted her with. It was while attending Franklin Pierce College she first began to nurture her love for the written word. As founder of Legacy of The Lotus fund, she works to raise funds for grassroots faith-based organizations involved in giving children of all ages much needed support in the community. She also works alongside survivors of trauma and tragedy as they realize their legacies through the writing of their own journeys.

✉ mysantana69@gmail.com

𝐟 www.facebook.com/femwhispers

𝐟 www.facebook.com/legacylotus

in www.linkedin.com/in/adriennesantana

𝒈+ www.google.com/+adriennesantana5

MANIFESTATION 23

State of the Heart

By Adrienne S. Santana

Early mornings are my most peaceful times of day—just before the sun breaks through the horizon and its warm rays top the trees. A cool breeze brushes softly across each blade of grass, still misted from midnight dew, giving rise to wonderfully delicious flavors of times passed. Memories of moments woven in love surround each of my senses as my heart becomes filled with gratitude and my walk with God rings in a new day with songs of birds. I like to believe as Adam walked through the Garden of Eden with God in the cool of the day, their time with one another must've been like my own moments with God. Not every morning is filled with joyful anticipation of what is to come. I have spent many times wrapped up in a past I did not understand or a future my heart truly wanted to avoid.

I believe in life. There is no soul or being closer to God than a child. I now understand how, as children grow older, the love of God becomes buried deep beneath the scars of pain and suffering. As a little girl growing up through trauma and tragedies, my heart's only desire was to be loved. Being separated from my mother and thrown into a whirlwind of extreme unpredictability and violence, I grew up never really knowing what was good and right, or how to become that beautiful little girl everyone adored. As I grew older, I spent much of my time observing other children my age. I watched as their mothers wrapped their arms around them and hugged them tightly and their fathers stood protectively over them. Every so often, I caught a glimpse of myself in those moments and my heart cried with a yearning to be a better girl, young woman, wife, and eventually a mother…to be loved "like that."

Everyone has a story to tell—their journey from darkness into light, a testimony of the power of God in their lives. With every step we take, a decision has been made, leaving behind a "footprint." Each footprint is a manifestation of the choices we made along the way. Looking back, my footprints seem to have gone in complete circles—I wandered through the wilderness in much the same way the Israelites must've while searching for their own promised land.

Over the years, I heard many of those old familiar expressions of wisdom passed down from generation to generation: *You are what you eat. As a man thinks in his heart, so is he. We speak from the abundance of our hearts.* I remember many times thinking to myself, *Yeah, yeah… great sayings, but that's not quite how life really works.* And then there were times of soft silence when I caught myself saying, "…or is it?"

Life eventually became busy for me, just as it does for anyone else. I married, had a child, divorced, began schooling, and started a career—catapulting me into the well-known "rat race" of big city life in Boston. There always seemed to be some crisis, some point in life where this unseen supernatural force threw a canyon across my path without the enormous warning signs and flashing yellow lights. I never did watch where I was walking and was often referred to as a clumsy child who tripped over her own feet, so I spent a lot of time free-falling from one crisis to the next—and not always my own. Actually, the majority of the crises I found myself in were because I felt the need or urge to run and save the day for someone who was hospitalized, suicidal, suddenly in need of shelter or food, or maybe their business, marriage, or children were in crisis. Whatever the crisis was, I was there to be calm, cool, collected, and to make things happen.

It took quite some time but I began realizing the truth behind all those phrases I'd heard over and over again—I even began speaking them myself. One of the more poignant opportunities in my life arose after having an emergency laparoscopy. A doctor walked into the recovery room where my mother sat at the end of my bed. He looked at me and simply said, "You are pregnant but the baby is very low and you may want to consider your options. I have seen young women in your situation before, and the baby never makes it." The news came as no surprise. I had already seen a couple of doctors, biopsies had been done, and I was given a diagnosis of cervical cancer. Now some may call it denial, but I call it a strong will and an incredible faith that God just did not want me to have cancer—but for whatever reason, he did want me to have a child. As this doctor stood over my bed telling me to think about my options, I didn't consider couth while telling him exactly what I thought of his opinion as I grabbed my clothes, making it clear I was going home.

I found an OB-GYN who would attend to me and my baby during my pregnancy—which was spent mostly on bed rest, with a few close calls of miscarrying. Each time, thoughts would enter my mind of how "that doctor was right, you're just gonna miscarry. It's never gonna happen." With every thought, tears would force their way to my eyes, but in my heart there was this demanding scream, "I WILL have a baby boy!" Sure enough, I had a beautiful son, weighing in at eight pounds, three and a half ounces. He was twenty-one inches long with soft tufts of red hair, and he's been my most prized gift for the last twenty-two years.

I've learned in life, trials and diverse temptations will arise and try our faith. Time is all that's required for patience to make her perfect work. While we do speak from the abundance of our hearts, it is the state of our heart that grants our desires and truly leaves us complete, entire, and in want of nothing. (James 1:2-4)

I have been battling for three years with severe nerve pain throughout my head, neck, and spine caused from three degenerated discs in my neck, but today I anticipate the final relief a surgery will bring. A surgery recently postponed due to a gall bladder attack, signaling a more urgent need. I'm filled with gratitude it happened now and not after my neck surgery, as it would have left me in a much worse condition than I am in currently. It's funny now, when I see through gratitude how our moments of crisis can actually be miracles in disguise. I am grateful for this pain, as it has become a friend of sorts, bringing me an appreciation for the life I live. An appreciation I'd never have known without it.

With long suffering, patience, and a continued conscious effort to come to this place of peace, I still have postcards hanging on every door, along with letter-sized posters placed in not-so-random areas, reminding me of the simplest affirmations. "I am worthy," "Patience makes her perfect work," and my favorite, by one of the most beautiful women I have ever known—my husband's mom and my spiritual mother—spoken with a soft giggle, "Let your words be sweet, so if they come back to you, they'll be easy to eat." There's a reason I call her for my daily dose of inspiration. I must say, in my experience, affirmations are rendered vain until my heart is open to receive from others. For it is through others God has delivered the love my heart always desired. I have learned through it all, it is not so much the person but the state of the heart I see and love. So, as a young girl, all I wanted was to be loved. Now as a woman, my heart's greatest desire is for those I love to know it. Now as I awake every morning, and circumstances arise throughout my day, I choose to meditate and walk with God in the cool of the day. I have learned if I can only keep my heart in a state of love and gratitude, I will no longer be a child or young woman wandering in circles, free-falling from crisis to crisis. I will be one who has found a love beyond compare, whose cup overflows with joy, and whose footprints are of a woman manifesting the desires of her heart—*in high heels*!

WENDY GAMBONE

Wendy Gambone has been an entrepreneur for more than fifteen years. She has owned and operated several businesses in the Katy area. Prior to entrepreneurship, she worked in the casino industry as well as the restaurant industry. Wendy earned her bachelor's degree in business administration at the age of thirty-seven—a personal goal that she felt was important to accomplish. Currently, Wendy runs the day-to-day operations of Tough Talk Network. Her greatest pride and joy and accomplishment are her family. She has been married to her best friend, Tony, for seventeen years and has three boys: Ryan, Anthony, and her stepson, Billy.

- www.facebook.com/wendy.gambone
- toughtalknetwork.com
- www.twitter.com/TTRNetwork
- WendyGambone@gmail.com

MANIFESTATION 24

$\mathcal{G}$T'S NOT WHAT HAPPENS TO US, IT'S WHAT HAPPENS FOR US

By Wendy Gambone

I've heard it said that things happen *for us* and not *to us*. Looking back on my life now, I realize how true a statement that is. At one time, however, I thought and felt that everything was happening *to me* and NEVER would have thought anything would happen *for me*.

Let me give you a little background. I am Wendy Gambone—wife, mother, daughter, sister, aunt, and believer. I am a southern girl who grew up mostly in Louisiana. By the time I was nineteen, I was married and had my first son, Ryan. There were definitely some struggles as a young wife and mother. If you ask me if being married and having children at that time was what I planned for my life, I would've told you I don't really know, because I often struggled with knowing what I wanted out of life. That struggle would last me for the majority of my life.

Fast-forward a few years—divorced at the ripe old age of twenty-one and living in Natchez, MS. I was taking college courses and working two jobs. After a while, it was too much so I decided to put college off. About this same time, it was announced that Natchez had been approved for gambling, and a riverboat casino made its way down the Mississippi River. Announcements came out that the casino, Lady Luck, was looking to hire dealers. I had never even been in a casino, much less worked in one, so it sounded pretty exciting. I was hoping I could support myself with one job so I could continue college.

The next step was to learn how to deal. Lady Luck had set up a location for a dealing school where they taught how to deal casino games. My dealing instructor was Tony Gambone from Philadelphia, by way of Las Vegas. Let's just say, having grown up in the South, I didn't meet too many men like Tony.

This is where my life with Tony started. We spent several years in the gaming business and eventually moved to Las Vegas. Tony and I were married in Las Vegas—no, it wasn't by Elvis. We had our son, Anthony, and decided it would be better to raise him closer to family, so we moved to Texas where my family lives. Prior to the gaming industry, Tony always worked for himself and had owned a remodeling business. When we moved, we started our business of remodeling kitchens and bathrooms. The business was great, and I loved every minute of it. It sustained us for many years. During this time, I was able to finally complete college—a big goal I had for a long time. Things were going great, life was good, the kids were good, and Tony and I were good. Good things were happening for us.

In August of 2008, our lives changed forever. I haven't told you that Tony suffered from Crohn's disease; there is no cause or cure. It's something he had since the age of nineteen. By the time we met, he had two surgeries and most of his bowel removed. From the time I met him in 1992 until 2008, he was healthy with no problems at all. When he began having pain bad enough to warrant a trip to the emergency room, you can imagine how terrified I was. Little did I know, this would turn into a five-year battle.

Let me back up a little and tell you about me. Growing up, my mom was very much into giving us the best life she could. Part of that for her was making sure we knew about God and what he had done for us. I pledged my life to Christ when I was fifteen. Unfortunately, by the time I was eighteen, all that had changed and I decided to live my life the way I wanted and did so for the next twenty years.

Those years weren't all bad, but from time to time I felt something was missing. It was early 2008 when I decided I wanted to go back to church. I decided on a local church, snuck in, and sat in the back row. The sermon was about fathers. I remember the preacher asking: "If something happened today to your husband, the father of your children, do you know if you would see him again in heaven?" That question hit me like a ton of bricks. I knew Tony believed in a higher power but he didn't really know who or what that higher power was. That very minute, I prayed that Tony would know Christ and that I would know for sure that if anything happened to him, I would see him again one day. I know God uses people, circumstances, and anything else he can to make us turn to him. I now know that God used Tony's illness to get me back to the life he wanted for me, and to get Tony's attention.

There was not one minute of those five years that was easy. I had no idea what to expect from day to day. At the time, I thought I had all these bad things happening *to me*. The fear I felt everyday was unbearable. I lost weight, I couldn't sleep, and I felt helpless. I began to pray daily that God would heal Tony and not allow him to die. After several visits to the hospital and doctor's office, Tony had to have a "minor" surgical procedure to drain an abscess. After that surgery, Tony ended up back in the hospital three days later with eight blood clots in his lungs. I had no idea before that day the severity of the situation, but I found out that many people don't survive. Later that night, we were told that he only had a 40 percent chance of surviving. This was the hardest time of my life. I started praying even more and asked everyone I knew to do the same.

We spent two full weeks in the hospital, but we made it! We were still dealing with his Crohn's, because the surgery did not rectify the problem like we hoped. For four years, no surgeon wanted to touch Tony because of the risks involved. Because of Tony having Crohn's, he was denied insurance coverage. In order for him to be covered by Medicare, he had to be on disability for two years. And I didn't mention that during this time of illness, we had to give up our business because Tony wasn't able to do the work. Once he got coverage, we found a doctor that was willing to perform surgery. By that time, my prayers had been answered and Tony was now a Christ follower and going to church with me regularly. It made all the difference in our lives. I can't explain how much of a difference this made, knowing we could really lean on God and our faith through that trying time. The difference before and after is just unexplainable.

When the surgeon said he could do the surgery, we were excited but I have to admit I was a little scared. I remember reading a verse in the Bible—James 5:14 – "Is anyone among you sick? Then he must call for the elders of the church and they are to pray over him, anointing him with oil in the name of the Lord…" So I asked Tony if he would let the pastors and staff of our church pray over him. He agreed and four days before surgery, they did. Our lead pastor, Mike, prayed and asked God to please let them open Tony up and find only dead disease and just have to clean it out and sew him back up. Tony and I will never forget that prayer.

Friday morning, on May 25, Tony went in for a six-hour surgery. I was a little anxious but nowhere near the fear and anxiety I had for the previous surgery—before I'd found peace again. Tony made it through surgery; God blessed us with an excellent surgeon. The next morning, making his rounds, the surgeon was happy to report it wasn't as bad as he thought. He said there was mostly dead tissue and he'd just had to clean it out. Well, I thought Tony was going to fall out of bed! We just looked at each other and smiled.

I look back now and see how all these thing have happened *for me* and not *to me*. For me to get to a better place with God. For me to get a better understanding of what this life is for, and for me to start a new business with Tony that helps others be successful. Throughout all this, I have learned it's not up to me to define my purpose in life but to let God define who I am and do it to the best of my ability. You wouldn't believe the relief of letting go of the struggle that comes with trying to figure out what you're supposed to do with your life. This doesn't mean you don't take action towards things—not at all. You just have to be open to anything and have faith that God will work through you to get there, wherever *there* is.

AUDREY L. WOODLEY, BS, MA

Audrey L. Woodley owns a professional networking company that empowers entrepreneurs through social media, private coaching, and personal development. Audrey wears many hats—founder of Changing Oasis, Inc. and Better Destination Media, Inc.—a social media PR boutique. Audrey has over fifteen years with educating and coaching. Audrey is the co-author of the book, *Network to Increase Your Net Worth*, and has successfully accomplished her five-day Chicagoland book tour and sold out each time. She has designed her own brand presence with The Beauty of Business Networking series, where business owners share brand and marketing success stories to help other professional women looking to start a successful business.

Let's stay connected!

plus.google.com/u/0/+AudreyWoodley/about

www.linkedin.com/in/audreywoodley

www.facebook.com/AlwoodleyCEO?ref=hl

www.instagram.com/audreywoodley

www.twitter.com/changingoasis

www.twitter.com/alwoodleyCEO

- www.pinterest.com/alwoodley
- www.blogtalkradio.com/fearlesseducatedwoman
- www.youtube.com/user/mzaudrey40
- www.audreywoodley.com
- audreywoodley@yahoo.com

MANIFESTATION 25

ᗡESIGNING MY DESTINY WITH CPR (CONDITION, PRAYER, REFLECTIONS)

By Audrey L. Woodley

With a dying savings account, my mother having only six months to live, and living out of fear, I felt as if I'd hit so many brick walls. I was literally having an identity crisis and had to come to terms with the fact that I was not ready to step out and be Audrey L. Woodley.

When I started my organization, Changing Oasis, I was looking forward to working with women who wanted to improve their leadership skills while building a support group where we could share resources and knowledge.

My goal was to become an author, and when the opportunity presented itself, I was able to show my talents and gifts with a five-day Chicagoland book tour. I built a platform about my business and how my life was transformed. With the joint venture, I was able to get more speaking opportunities and gain more visibility for my brand. Now, I am a self-published co-author and coach women with their business via Blog Talk Radio, workshops, and private coaching. I knew that this venture would hit it big, but then came the news about my mother—my rock, my best friend—she was everything to me. I found out she had been battling cancer. Everything stopped. I couldn't even think about a book launch, much less anything else.

I spent several years trying to hit the mark and make it big: I tried real estate, a second-hand retail store, several home-based businesses. All I got was less money in my savings account, which was already at zero. There were no team members, co-partnerships, or support. But then I made an investment in my joint venture with Toni Coleman to write my story and use my networking skills to build my brand and my business. Unfortunately, I hit another brick wall and I had no control over it. I spiraled downward with nothing to hold on to. I was devastated. But eventually, I found something to hold onto…my faith and worship.

Situations you are faced with on a daily basis can leave you unable to breathe. We must remember not to be a victim of our circumstance—or anyone's circumstance. Prayer is the connection that you have with the Holy Spirit. This is the time when you turn on the music that feeds your soul. Open up your Bible, open up your mouth, and worship God. Your worship is the most supernatural thing that someone can experience with our heavenly father. Do not let anyone take you from that connection.

In order to grow and move to the next level God has for you, you can reflect with journaling. Write down the lesson God shows you, and see how living in today's uncertain times can be used to push you forward. I often find myself on the edge, short-tempered, and reckless. But through these perilous times, I have to pull my resources and reach into my spiritual basket to snap myself back together. I have decided to live a drama-free life, but as always, you often have to face one trial after another. We all have to live with death, divorce, sickness, pain, joblessness, and fake friends. God can touch those situations that you had no business dealing with in the first place. These conditions can leave you paralyzed. Begin to write down the takeaways, and more importantly, share your testimony to help and heal others, because God gets the glory. Amen!

When you think of the term CPR, what are the first things or thoughts that come to mind? Naturally, you think someone is hurt, unable to breathe, experiencing helplessness, and in need of mouth-to-mouth resuscitation, and may even need someone to use a defibrillator to bring them back to life. So it is the same with *spiritual* CPR. Below are seven steps of CPR:

I.   Know your worth - Psalm 40:1-2

II.   Know your vision - Jeremiah 29:11

III. Know your faults - Philippians 2:3-4

IV.   Forgive yourself - Genesis 33:4

V.   Plan your goals - John 16:13

VI.   Live your dreams - Hebrews 11:1

VII. Walk into your purpose - Luke:39-42

Live, breathe, resuscitate, bring back to life, revive, and allow someone to help you see the value of your life.

Sometimes life's challenges hit you so damn hard you think you're in a nightmare, but you have to deal with every curve ball that comes your way. I have been on my own yearlong battle of staying mentally sane in this nightmare.

I have been faced with taking care of my mother's business after her passing in 2013. There was no clear direction, but I knew my mother wanted me to take care of my grandmother. I have been attacked by family members, and many do not support or care what I have been going through. This is a tough place to be in. All I know is the pain and stress one goes through when taking care of an elderly person, supporting someone with a bad habit, and burying a loved one all at the same time can leave you feeling lifeless.

I have been called a fraud and pushed into a corner of questioning my integrity and leadership ability. When you are left in charge of someone's estate and left to be a beneficiary, you have to be ready for all that comes with being the heir.

My spiritual background comes in with the faith hat called CPR. I created this system to be able to take on life's challenges and to be able to breathe—in spite of all the stress, trials, and curve balls that have come my way.

My version of CPR is a seven-step spiritual system designed by me based on condition, prayer, and reflection. This system was given to me by God, to help me stay focused when life felt too hard to bear.

As I mentioned above, there are seven steps of spiritual CPR. Each step will have a condition, you'll have to pray about it, and then release and reflect on it.

KNOW YOUR WORTH:

How many times have you been in a relationship and felt like you always got the short end of the stick? Or how many times have you wanted to develop your own program and never had the money to invest in it? So often, we get caught in the same rut and keep going back to those same excuses, but we can't seem to figure out the WHY. If we can take back the decision we made early on, we wouldn't feel desperate for a man, or bitter because our friend started the same company we wanted and now she's doing her thing.

This is when CPR comes in.

What is the condition? We weren't prepared for the relationship or the business. As of matter of fact, my life was a wreck, and any situation at the time would have fallen to pieces because I just wasn't ready. This is when we withdraw and start to believe what we see. This is when the second part, prayer, comes in.

The prayer: God, I know my worth, and I accepted anything to come into my life, and know, Lord, I need you now. I need you to take my hand and show me your direction. I've tried to do it myself over and over, and my plate is empty and I'm broken. I know I deserve better.

Now it's time for reflection. We all have issues or problems we face at the end of the day, and sometimes you can't just do it by yourself. In this case, reflect on the scripture and the word God gives you to excel in life. God gives us million-dollar ideas and daily downloads, and we have to begin manifesting those ideas and without getting distracted from our divine order. Accept the challenge and prepare for what God has in store for you.

CPR has changed so many lives—even college students use it for their personal guide to help them during their trials and tribulations in school. There is no limit to what you can manifest through your faith...and continuous use of spiritual CPR. Feel free to create your own CPR for your daily life challenges. Remember, you are not alone!

If you'd like to know more about CPR, or Changing Oasis, please connect with me.

LUV ALSTON, RN, BA, CPC

Founder/CEO of Luv Is The Word. An Alchemist and creator of Agape Intelligence (AI), Luv possesses a gift for deeply connecting with people at laser speed, helping others do the same. A professor, radio host, RN, certified coach, and speaker, Luv is an international best-selling author; She worked full time as a single mom until marrying her bestie, Gary.

Luv shares her calling using principles of AI with women, internationally. She is a lively and experienced keynote speaker. Her gift creates a warm, fun environment to empower women's lives and workplaces.

✉ luvleighalston@gmail.com

⌂ stoa.vpweb.com

🐦 Luv Is The Word @peters12Nikki

▶ www.youtube.com Luv Is The Word

MANIFESTATION 26

BEING UNAPOLOGETICALLY, AUTHENTICALLY YOU

By Luv Alston

The first step in being your most authentic self is realizing that *you matter*! What you think, feel, create, and experience matters. Second, embracing your choice of *you* is one of the most precious and important gifts you possess! Even angels weren't gifted with freedom of choice — or high heels, for that matter. This gift of choice allows you into the high heels of being authentically you — imperfect perfection. Authenticity is about claiming authorship, often through a process of unearthing your most genuine, true, real, and undoubted self.

I'm an alchemist. I love and find joy in understanding how people relate and how we experience our environment and world. When I think over my life, I realize that I've always been this. Something I've found odd is how we imprint on one another, from birth, in some unhealthy ways. We often see the world, environment, and others as happening *to us* once we become young adults. Yet, we refuse to be accountable for the part we played in choosing *not to choose* or going along to get along.

I want to be clear — babies and children are a very powerful force in the effects they impose on their environment. And yet they are dependent on the adults in their lives for food, shelter, clothing, love, care, and a greater sense of self and purpose as they grow. I had the incredible fortune to be raised from a few weeks old until nearly eight years old by my grandparents on an island where I was related to, and in relationship with, nearly everyone — the isle of Beaufort, NC. By the time my grandparents were raising me, they were their most authentic selves. They took the time to learn whom I was and cultivated my gifts and talents, all while surrounding me with love, care, discipline, and spirituality. They imprinted on me the need to have great relationships with the almighty universe, others, my environment, and myself. They imprinted compassion and empathy for others, while remaining true to my most authentic self.

On occasion, I saw my birth parents, and though my grandmother tried to explain the chick coming through the door was my mother, I never could feel it or grasp it—not with her or my birth father, especially when I had to go live with them. They too tried to imprint on me and some things got through, such as working, reading others, having an unquenchable thirst to know more.

I realize now, their method of imprinting (their belief of who they wanted me to be for them and worse, that who I was didn't matter), included emotional, mental, and physical torture. Because neither understood being their most authentic self, as many people are intimidated by authenticity! I became impervious to their meaner attempts to imprint. I understand now it was easier for things to be a certain way, including their lives.

Your most authentic you requires the courage to do intense self-study. I'm telling you this because it's important to understand that being your most authentic self also requires patience, desire, ability to choose your behaviors, and to work through your fears of rejection, abandonment, and people pleasing. Your authentic self needs your consistent courage and diligence to emerge! Many women tell me they feel as though they lost themselves to children, spouses, family, friends, their job, and the world. What they're really saying is they are choosing to get with someone else's idea of who they should be! This becomes comfortable though, often leaving them unhappy, depressed, and unable to find joy.

Now I know and understand that when doubts whisper my name, when storms rage and fears call out to me, it's a sign that I'm evolving to my next level of love and understanding, growth, and deeper self-development. When I feel pain, suffering, and treated unfairly without care for my personhood, it's time to become still and learn the lessons my heart is attempting to teach me about compassion in the face of cruel, unusual behaviors. When I face my personal demons of hurt and wrath with calm and courage, I know I'm heading to be a blessing to others.

When I can embrace my perfect imperfections and announce, "Damn, I'm a boss-ass chick!" I put on my high heels, and I once more manifest my most authentic self.

Once we realize that there's no need to apologize for being a woman, a gift, a light and fabulous being, we are tapping into our authenticity! Authenticity propels us beyond what others and ourselves are comfortable being! It stretches, prunes, deepens, and upends subconscious beliefs. Authenticity drives us beyond our fears of rejection, allowing us the courage to give and receive agape—love unconditionally.

How does one obtain this magical elixir? What are the steps to let go of those behaviors that no longer serve us? How do we reach this ability to transform our minds through balance into an ability to abolish our own "upper limiting" behaviors and emerge as our most brilliant, authentic selves? How do we put on our high heels and step into the world, knowing we are worthy, brilliant, and beautiful?

AI is the solution…as an alchemist, creating Agape Intelligence, for me, is about more than having relationships. It's about going through the paces and learning how to *choose* healthy, happy relationships. In AI, I developed a scientific, spiritual, emotional, and physical solution, so that we feel what we feel, experience emotions, and find freedom in learning to choose behaviors where we arrive at our intended outcome.

AI molds itself to the needs of the individual, family unit, or group. Science has shown that at times your feelings and emotions serve you, the outcome you desire, and empathy toward the surrounding environments you affect. At other times, you learn to feel what you do and then act opposite to emotion or feelings, as they may not serve you in every instance.

AI is a house, and its foundation is self-study, self-control, and behavioral management. We spend much of our time using tools and techniques I developed to build your skills of authenticity, feeling what you do while choosing behaviors that provide the outcome you want. We work on empathy and cultivating and maintaining only *your* choice in happy, healthy relationships. And you learn the basics of body language, building boundaries based heavily on what you do want. Most importantly, you learn how to love on you, for you, with daily practices. You learn that you are beautiful, magnificent, brilliant, loving, caring, fun, and — like me — a boss-ass chick in the flyest high heels.

You can learn the skills, tools, and techniques to thrive beyond your past into your gift of a stunning, authentic life. And it will require hard self-work — and I promise some fun and hilarity, too. You will need to make choices, learn from your opportunities for growth (i.e., pain, suffering, experiences, joys, happiness, sadness, hate, and most importantly, love). The question is: can you accept that in order to step into and walk into and through your most authentic life, you have to listen to your heart with courage? Can you accept that excavating the marvel that is really and truthfully you requires care, time, and is a daily process?

Whatever struggle or pain, AI equips me with the ability to enjoy the process, take in the lessons, and stand in the blessing of being my most authentic self! You too can live in a new reality of healthy, happy relationships with yourself. I created AI for you! You matter, and you're important!

LINDSEY F. RAINWATER

Lindsey Rainwater is a Divine Gifts coach and is also known as the Archangel's Emissary. She educates people on how to discover their spiritual gifts, as well as how to embrace them. She also helps her clients to cleanse, heal, and protect themselves from negative energy and emotions.

Last but not least, she helps to get people in touch with their angels and brings across the messages that angels have for us. You can get more information on her services, along with a free Divine Gifts meditation by visiting http://lindseyrainwater.com

www.facebook.com/lindseyrainwaterangels

www.twitter.com/LindseyAngels

www.youtube.com/user/thelindseyrainwater

www.linkedin.com/pub/lindsey-rainwater/3b/653/7a4

Lindsey@lindseyrainwater.com

lindseyrainwater.com

MANIFESTATION 27

SUPERCHARGE YOUR MANIFESTATIONS BY TRUSTING YOUR ANGELS

By Lindsey F. Rainwater

Trust is not easy. It isn't something that is easy to get, and it isn't easy to give. We've all experienced being burned by someone at some point—someone we put our faith in, someone we found lacking in one way or another.

Trust is a difficult subject when you're dealing with palpable, flesh-and-blood beings whom you can take hold of, look in their eyes, and discern whether they're going to do what you need them to, or if they're going to drop the ball.

When you start thinking about placing trust in a force that can't be weighed or measured, it's understandable that your brain wants to have a meltdown.

But trusting in the huge divine powers that surround us is exactly what we need—because that source is the only one that will steer us right, every time.

One of the best examples of this is your angels. Everybody has them, and they want to help you with everything you need. All you have to do is ask for their assistance and trust they are bringing you what you need.

Being human, we have this thing called the ego. It's what makes us who we are, but it also has a terrible habit of getting in our way and tripping us up. It's that little voice in your mind that starts yammering away, telling you that you should be worried, that you need to plan more, and that you need to know exactly how everything is going to happen.

Over the last couple years, I've started seeing how much my ego can really screw me over—even though it seems to just want me to slow down and be logical. The other side of this is that I've been taught a huge lesson in trust and letting go of attachments—and seeing the amazing things that come of it.

The first example I can think of is when I really wanted to go to a book writing/publishing workshop. I desperately wanted to get to this event, and my husband fully supported it, but we really didn't have the funds to send me.

The amount of money required to get to this event was large enough that I simply couldn't micromanage how that money was going to come. So I said, "It will happen if it's supposed to happen." I asked God and the angels to bring me the funds to go to this event if I was meant to go. Then I continued with life, busying myself with other things and trusting everything was going to work out.

Sure enough, a couple windfalls of money came our way, and while it wasn't a lot, it was enough to send me on my trip. On top of that, someone going to the same event offered to let me stay with her, so I didn't even have to get a room.

Ever since then, I've tried to let go of my ego's need to plan and control every little thing, although I haven't always been successful.

In fact, it wasn't long ago that I panicked about money coming into my business. I lost a revenue stream that had basically been keeping my business afloat while I was making some changes and creating the business model I have now. Instead of trusting that everything was going to be fine and asking my angels to help me manifest the money I needed, I started focusing on manifesting some freelance writing work—something I had given up doing a long time ago because it didn't resonate with me.

A freelancing gig did come my way, and I was thrilled because it would give me the money I thought I needed. So I succeeded in manifesting what I wanted, but forgot that it wasn't what I needed.

Everything fell apart after that. I had some personal issues (code: morning sickness) that made life difficult for me, but overall I just shut down. I didn't want to work on this project. It didn't take me further down my divine path, and it certainly wasn't fun, so my spirit rejected it.

I think some part of me was saying, "You left this because it drains you, and now you're back! What are you thinking?"

I fell into a depression and only completed half the project. Thankfully, the client was thrilled with the half I did, but I was ashamed and embarrassed that I couldn't pull enough brain cells and spirit together to finish what I started. The project fizzled to an end, and he took the rest of it elsewhere.

Pulling out of the depression took weeks—I lost about a month. I simply cannot recall it. It was only in talking daily to my angels and focusing on the positive life changes that were coming around the bend, that I was able to raise myself out of it.

But it left me wondering, "What the heck just happened to me?" Pregnancy was a part of it, I'm sure, but it wasn't the whole story.

So I released my fears, worries, and stress, and retreated into my mind for a little one-on-one time with my entourage—my angels and my higher self. I asked what I'd done wrong, and because I wanted an honest answer, I got one.

They told me, "You stopped trusting that we have everything in hand, and that everything is perfect. When you stopped trusting in us, you felt that everything was on you. Since you are imperfect, you knew you couldn't handle the kind of responsibility you were trying to place on yourself. So you shut down."

As you can probably imagine, that was eye-opening.

Since then, I've been working hard. I had a move to make, I had my health and the health of my growing child to keep track of, and I had a business to run. So I have been doing everything that I feel is my responsibility to do.

When the angels give me a directive, I follow it—including being in this book.

What I am not doing is worrying about how things are going to come about. I'm not trying to plan out more than I feel is my responsibility to plan, and I'm not questioning whether everything is going to turn out all right.

I trust my angels to bring me everything I need and more, and even in the past few days, I have seen them work wonders.

As I moved, I told the angels I knew they had brought me here for a good reason, and I had high hopes for this community. But I don't have a network here, so I asked them to bring someone into my sphere who would appreciate the work I do and be a great contact to get me into the community.

I held that intention—of being well-received into the community, and to find a group of people who were enthusiastic about my skills. But I didn't put any parameters on how this would come about, or what these people would be like.

Two days later, I went to run an errand, only to discover the store I was going to didn't open for another hour. It was odd I had forgotten that detail, so I reached out and asked, "Well, now what?"

The answer was, "Time for a walk."

I headed down the street, taking in the stores, all of which were still closed. I wasn't sure where I was going, but I knew they would tell me when I arrived. After a few blocks, I came by a shop that looked interesting. I didn't think much of it until I was about to pass by, and I heard, "Look closely. Take a good look."

The sign said open. At that point, I was almost past it, but I could feel myself being drawn inside. Long story short, the owner was the coolest person you could meet, and within thirty minutes of chatting, she was calling me her "soul sister."

I was overjoyed. I had listened to my angels' directions. She has been in the community for a long time and has a great network who will be interested in my services. But I was also thrilled that I hadn't created any attachments regarding what my new contact would be like, because this woman wouldn't have been it.

I feel like the very best advice I could give anyone is to simply learn how to trust once you set your manifestation in motion, then follow the directives you receive.

Manifestation is a journey—like the rest of life—and we're never "done" with it. Once you start manifesting, it's something you keep doing in order to turn your life into what you want it to be.

Be confident in asking for what you want and putting your intentions out into the Universe. But don't put too many stipulations on it. Focus on the result, and leave the rest up to the Universe and your angels. That is when you will see the most powerful and unexpected manifestations occur.

LAURIE CROOKELL, BA

Creative spark. Unique ideas. Rich imagination. Born to write. These are a few of the words people use to describe Laurie Crookell. An international best-selling author, writer, and speaker, Laurie feels deeply moved by the emotive power of words.

Holding a BA in economics, she provides one-on-one math and literacy support for children with learning differences, motivating others to utilize their struggles as a catalyst to live happier and more fulfilled lives.

Laurie also owns a freelance writing company, Where Words Are Art. Her writing has been recognized in numerous writing competitions for essays, prose, and children's fiction.

- www.facebook.com/laurie.crookell
- www.facebook.com/LaurieCrookellAuthor
- lauriecrookell@shaw.ca
- www.lauriecrookell.com
- www.linkedin.com/pub/laurie-crookell/52/37/859
- www.twitter.com/LaurieCrookell
- www.youtube.com/channel/UChLMMzsyFh1DCqHRnJ9rCcw

ℋ MOTHER'S QUEST: CHOOSING TO BELIEVE BEYOND IMPOSSIBLE

By Laurie Crookell, BA

Raindrops drum against my bedroom window, moving to the beat of their own rhythm in time and space. Striking the glass at diverse intervals, seemingly infinite, incalculable by time. This is the pulse of my daughter's mind, the way it is wired, the vibration to which she responds. Absorbing stimuli from sights, sounds, thoughts, and feelings at heightened speeds from everything and everyone around her. This is her life…living with autism.

She's "high-functioning"—at the top of the autism spectrum. Meaning her autism is invisible to most but a few, which actually means *she* is invisible to most but a few. A young girl no different than another, imbued with talents and intellect beyond the norm. She thinks. She feels. She laughs. She cries. She comprehends. But others do not comprehend her, her self-expression inhibited by the challenges of autism spectrum disorder.

Our terminology infers she has a "disorder"—a word that screams limitation. Some prefer the term disease, hoping one day, a cure will be found. But what if it's our perception that's the disease? What if she is more than a disorder? What if the answer lies within our embrace of those perceived differences?

I trudged along the dull, linoleum floor of my daughter's school, worry's shadow tagging behind. Her teacher's words echoed through my mind, mirroring the hollow echo of my footsteps.

"Your daughter's learning is very behind," her teacher had said. "Perhaps she should be in a special-needs school."

I nodded at the advice given to me countless times before. Same old story. If a child didn't fit the norm, they were deemed a "slow learner"—a misfit. I sighed, fear and worry etching lines across my forehead. How could I help others see her for who she was? How would I help them understand that she simply *learned* differently? My frustration mingled with anger, worry, and exhaustion, creating a daunting Mount Everest-sized task in my mind.

She was my daughter. My firstborn. Beautiful. Precocious. Lively. Dynamic. Inspiring. She danced to the beat of her own unique rhythm. A rhythm few understood but I. Yet it was a rhythm marked with striking grace. Hope defined who she was. If I removed hope from the equation, she would be lost.

Her visual genius exhibited itself early, when she taught herself how to walk. At nine months old. No inching along the furniture. No wobbly practice sessions with me holding her hands. She figured it out herself. Scrutinizing other children. Observing the mechanics. Analyzing it. Then one evening, she stood up and walked across the room.

By the age of one, she could outrun me, shocking people with her speed. She jumped like a frog, ran like a deer, climbed like a spider monkey, and swung from monkey bars like a chimpanzee—swift, agile, strong. All learned by watching other children for only a few minutes. Gymnastics and dance classes proved the same. Show her the routine once…she had it, no matter how intricate the steps.

Her sheer speed captivated and amazed, visually problem-solving faster than most adults. In seconds, she could untangle the most complex of knots in a rope that had wound its way around a toy.

The standing joke among friends was that she would be Canada's first female prime minister. Yet her language skills did not develop at the same speed. For years, my concerns were dismissed. It was likely due to her early childhood trauma, I was told. But by the age of ten, she was diagnosed with ASD (Autism Spectrum Disorder).

School presented a never-ending challenge for her. Traditional teaching methods relied on auditory learning, but my daughter was not only visual, her auditory processing was significantly challenged. This had nothing to do with her hearing, rather the way her brain processed what her ears heard. Unable to filter out background noise, all sound competed equally for her attention, the sound of caterpillars crawling, spiders spinning webs, the buzz of ladybug wings—all magnified sounds most people didn't notice.

She also struggled to distinguish sounds. Where others heard distinct and separate phonemes in words, she heard blurs. One day, we walked past a river. It gurgled over rocks and rushed downstream. We stopped, drinking in nature's peace. "Mom," she said, "that's how I hear sound. When people talk to me. That's what I hear. Not the individual sounds of each word. A sound like a rushing river. It's like a blur."

When her differences were accepted and understood, she thrived. When misjudged and rejected, she withdrew into her autism, anxiety rising up like a dragon from the depths of earth, yearning to protect herself.

Rigidity as to how things had to be done stifled her natural talents, while triggering that dragon within, her anxiety a crippling power that overwhelmed. Yet when open-mindedness prevailed and new approaches adopted, she rose to the challenge. Formal public speaking was one such area of extreme anxiety. So one teacher allowed her to give a class presentation as a question-and-answer session instead—it relaxed her anxiety. She exceeded expectations, fully engaged the class, and showcased her natural brilliance. Her teacher's willingness to adapt to her needs set her up for success, encouraging her to reach for further success.

She was an out-of-the box thinker, unable to fit inside the box. She struggled to organize herself, struggled to remember due dates, struggled to understand verbal instructions. And yet, this was also part of her gift, as evidenced during her first high school art class. An assignment to paint a flower elicited the typical myriad of roses, daffodils, orchids, and lilies.

My daughter produced a carnivorous, Amazonian-type flower from the future, created entirely from her mind. Petals danced in the wind, colors seizing the viewers' attention and luring them to the flower's core. The edges of the petals on one side wilting as man's destructive force crept in on the flower's natural beauty. A depth of meaning painted with each brushstroke. She dared to challenge the norm. Dared to push beyond.

Her mind showed an equal ability to think outside the box. For her, life was about the pursuit of knowledge, discovery, invention, and breakthrough. The unknown beckoned her. A rare intellect she had, supported by an insatiable curiosity. How did things work? How did clouds move across the sky? What was the driving force behind quantum physics? Why? Why? Why?

Yet her thought process continued to be far beyond her verbal expression. Though her speech sounded fine on the surface level, finding the words to effectively verbalize the depth of her ideas frustrated her endlessly.

At sixteen, she determined that all conscious behavior sprang from our subconscious beliefs and thoughts. So if we wanted to change our behavior patterns, we first needed to change our subconscious beliefs. She was only sixteen and likely figured this out by age fourteen, before finding the words to orally explain it.

This same child, who struggled to learn how to read and write, later became an A student in English, writing stories and essays that astounded. She devoured books on quantum physics, eagerly studied the philosophical works of Nietzsche, Lao Tzu, and Confucius...and managed to write a 100 percent college philosophy exam. But her intelligence went beyond. Never content to simply memorize things in school (in fact, memorizing facts was a struggle for her), she wanted to know the *why, how,* and *what if,* happily spending hours in the library researching her questions. She innately understood patterns, seeing the bigger picture in even mundane things that would be ignored by many.

Some called her autistic. I called her an old soul. Thoughtful, introspective, a seeker of knowledge, highly inquisitive, intelligent, uninterested in status and wealth. From the mouths of earth's ancient souls flows the wisdom we seek. The question is: Are we ready to hear?

"Humans have used mirrors for as long as anyone can at least be aware of. We see in each other what we see in ourselves. And we judge others by the same basis in which we would judge ourselves." (Quote by my daughter, aged seventeen.)

Every mother has a dream. A dream that is universally the same: to watch our children grow into responsible, productive, successful, happy adults. I, too, shared this dream. Many did not believe it possible. Sometimes, I doubted it myself.

Yet manifesting my dream simply presented new opportunities for growth. It meant training myself not to be led by the limiting beliefs of others. If I viewed her in the manner others did, she would fulfill my limitations. If instead, I viewed her as having the infinite possibility of accomplishing whatever she chose to do, she would rise and become as I potentially saw her. This is not to say there are not challenges. Nor does it mean we ignore those challenges. It merely means we shift our focus.

Her hope lay in my trust, in my optimism, in my undying belief in her *ability*, not her disability. Our thoughts are the foundation upon which our lives are built. If only everyone understood who she was…a gift from ancient souls beyond the realms of earth.

My daughter is now twenty years old. Her story continues to unfold today, as she works on manifesting the life of her own dreams.

CHRISTINE MARMOY

Christine Marmoy, innovative and creative edge marketing mentor, passionately inspires women in business worldwide to unleash their innovative edge to boost visibility, build credibility, and get more clients through publishing their own best seller.

Christine is also the compiler and publisher of the international best-sellers, *Success in (High) Heels* and *Hot Mama in (High) Heels*. Her own inspirational book, *These Dreams Are Made for Walking*, provides women (and men) the guidelines to make their dreams a reality and to be unstoppable in life and business through her success workout, which was released in 2013, and was also a best seller. All the books published by Coaching & Success have hit the best-seller list within a few hours of publication.

Because that's what we do! We don't just publish books...we create best sellers!

🏠 www.coachingandsuccess.com

🏠 www.thewomensedgemag.com

🏠 www.successinhighheels.com

f www.facebook.com/coachingandsuccess

MANIFESTATION 29

Give – THANK – WELCOME

By Christine Marmoy

Following my very personal and quite extraordinary encounter with the Universe a few years ago, I have exhaustively researched how this connection could be maintained, forged even deeper and, most importantly, how it could produce the same results over and over again — regardless of who was using the process. I was certainly very curious but also very fearful of losing it at the same time! This latter feeling is the very reason why most of us have sporadic, unsustainable results. The fear of *losing it all* implies that you do not trust in the belief that you'll always be provided for. By default, if you gain something, it can always be lost at any time, without warning. At least, our human brain — the left side — likes to believe that. But, of course, me being me, I wanted it all and still do every day.

Along the path I have taken, I have certainly encountered ups and downs in manifesting my successes. But I have never again experienced downs plummeting to absolute zero since that magical day. However, I could see the flow was unreliable. Why was I able to manifest huge achievements very quickly while struggling with less important ones, despite all my efforts? That's the question I will try to answer for you within these few pages. For sure, it's great to be able to manifest something, but believe me, it's a lot more satisfying when you know deep down, at the very core of your heart and soul, that you can manifest anything you wish...at any time.

Just imagine in your head right now what your life would be like if you had such power? What would you be doing? Where would you be? What would you get rid of? What would you welcome into your life? Now, move that thought a bit deeper into your heart, and when you answer each of the questions above, what is your heart truly saying to you? What feeling comes to you first? (Write it down without disconnecting yourself from the feeling.). What do you feel in your body? Is it expanding? Did you suddenly feel lighter? What comes right after that? What is the second feeling? Is it fear, anxiety, depression? What is your body experiencing? — a contraction in your solar plexus, heartache, dizziness? Is your heart trying to win some kind of race?

This second feeling is the fracture point. This is how many of us manage to reduce, or even completely annihilate, our power. Faith — the binding cement in your manifesting process; it is what will keep the flow coming to you, stronger and stronger over time, until this small river transforms itself into a very quiet but significant torrent. If you are afraid it will stop, this means you have stepped away from faith…in which case, yes, it *will* stop.

So how do you maintain that faith? Even better, how do you make it deeper and reinforce it so it's so strong your fears won't even get close to it anymore?

Faith is blind and, of course, doesn't require any sort of proof; however, it's a lot better if you can receive some encouragement along the way, especially in the beginning. I have a very simple 1-2-3 formula that I still use today, because it works very well. However, these days I have added a few elements to that original formula. I will focus mainly on these little points because I know they will make a real difference in your own manifesting routine.

GIVE AND YOU SHALL RECEIVE!

Every time I had money coming into my account, I used to tithe an amount. I still do and if you do as well, then please don't stop! It is a very powerful manifesting secret. No matter how little money you have, tithe at least 10 percent of what you have every month.

Consistency in your giving seems to be way more important than the actual amount you give.

However, there is a direct relationship between what you give and what you receive. For example, if you give your *time* to a church or organization every week while trying to manifest more *money* in your business, it won't work. Why? Because the two are different. Imagine two buckets—when you give your time to your community, you are adding energy to the "time" bucket, so in exchange you can only receive *more time*—because that's the only bucket you contributed to.

In other words, if you want more money, you must contribute to the *money* bucket.

The idea is that you need to give first to be able to receive. And you will only get paid back in terms of what you gave away in the first place. You pay your contribution in love, you get back more love. You pay your contribution in time, you get back more time. That is how the Universe works.

I know you are probably saying, "Oh, but I don't give to expect something in return. I give because I *want* to give." If so, great. That is a noble way of thinking in the human world, but it's not the right way as far as the Universe is concerned. Just because some human beings decided you should give and never expect to receive does not mean it's right! Actually, it was an excellent method of keeping people in a state of poverty for a very long time. Being able to receive—and even more so, *expecting* to receive—are crucial elements in the manifesting process, without which you can only fail.

How many times have you said or heard somebody say: "I keep giving but it never comes back to me....but, oh well, it's OK because I don't expect anything."

Well, there you have it! The Universe is just following what you are asking for—you *want* to give and you *don't want* to receive....and the Universe always listens to us and does what we tell it to do.

You'll have to come to terms with and live in peace with that new state of mind. You'll have to embrace the notion of receiving. Use affirmations in the beginning to help you feel comfortable with this new way of being. Then move on to meditation (still continuing with the affirmations); meditation will bring you peace of mind, which is a prerequisite to manifesting. And soon, you'll become a good, heart-centered receiver. Being able to receive is not bad. It doesn't make you greedy, selfish, or self-indulgent. When you offer something to somebody, if they don't show you their appreciation, if you don't see that your gift made them happy, it saddens you, right? And you may not be inclined to buy another gift for that person. Well, it's exactly the same thing with the Universe. You need to show your appreciation, and the best way to show it is with the expectation of being heard and being willing to receive with love what you have asked for with love.

So, remember...give first and pay for it in the currency of what you want to receive.

THANK AND YOU SHALL RECEIVE!

By the same token, having just shared with you that it's necessary to always give prior to receiving, the same applies to *thanking* before the expected manifestation actually occurs in your physical reality. Thanking the Universe for having heard your request and for actively working on the delivery process is not a lie! I know some people feel very uncomfortable with this part because they feel they are just being foolish and lying to themselves. The only one you are fooling and lying to while thanking the Universe *prior to receiving* is your EGO! When you ask something of somebody, don't you automatically say "thank you"? Of course you do—firstly because you have good manners but also because you know the answer will be forthcoming, so you thank that person in advance. Do you ever feel as if you are cheating or lying when being polite? I doubt it very much!

So, why wouldn't you do the same with the Universe? Why would it be any different with the life force that created it all and is inside everything and everyone of us? In other words, why wouldn't you thank YOU?

There are a few things I do every day—no matter what! It's part of my routine of being grateful. Being able to thank the Universe means being grateful for everything that has already materialized in your world. Thank the Universe as soon as you wake up. Actually, the first thought I have is, "Thank you, Universe, for everything in my life." Then when I get up, I usually thank it for everything I do. Thank you to the Universe for this delicious cup of coffee. Thank you to the Universe for this tasty breakfast. Thank you to the Universe for the good night I had, etc. You get the idea? Yes, for sure, if I was to thank the Universe out loud, among people who don't know me, they'd probably think I'd lost the plot. That idea actually makes me smile. The thought that people would think I'm not all there because I am thanking the Universe for everything is quite odd, don't you agree? Especially if I was in a bad mood, complaining about everything under the sun, it would probably sound quite normal to these same people. So, feel free to say it in your head...just make sure you feel the true meaning of it. You really need to feel grateful.

After I am done thanking the Universe, I move on to my gratitude journal. I'm sure some of the other co-authors will share about this, so I'm not going to go into great detail here. I just like to write down, in a beautiful book, everything I'm grateful for that has already come about in my physical reality, or that I know is already there in the field surrounding me. Because once you've thought it, it's created! Sometimes I write a lot, sometimes not so much—there really is no hard and fast rule; it depends on the time I have available in the morning. Sometimes I start in the morning and finish at the end of my day. Some people like to do it in the evening. My point is you can be flexible. Don't let the format hold you back—just do it and do it every day.

Remember, thank first and you open the gate.

WELCOME IN ACTIONS!

Needless to say, giving, asking, and learning to receive will not serve any purpose if you do not *act* upon your wish! You have to walk the talk. However, that walk is usually a lot easier when you first give, ask, and open your mind to receive. Otherwise, you'll only be working from the outside, from your WILL. And, yes, that works sometimes, but I can tell you two things—one, it's not fast; and two, it's the hardest way. I know that firsthand because I've been there and done the same thing for many years.

You need to really understand that anything you already see in your material world has not been created out of this physical world. It has been created within the realm of the Universe's energy. Then and only then was it delivered into the world of physicality. Once you fully grasp this concept, not from an intellectual standpoint but from an emotional and conscious viewpoint, you'll be able to manifest anything into your life.

Now, it's not because the Universe handles the bulk of the work that there is nothing for you to do—quite the opposite, in fact. If you don't do anything, it will still be created because the Universe always does the work, but it won't appear in your reality. Instead, it will be piled up in your "savings" account out there in the field, where all the other things you asked for but never worked to materialize are stored—until you decide to do the work.

Let me explain to you what this "work" part looks like when you sign up for a partnership with the Universe. As soon as you give, thank, and welcome what your heart desires, it is created. Quantum physics has proved this many years ago...so there is no way of denying it. Now your work is to do what it takes to materialize the created desire into your own reality. Remember, I said it would be easier? That's because the Universe will start sending you clues, pointers, ideas—like falling flakes of snow. You'll see more and more synchronicity in your life, and events and circumstances will take place to facilitate the concrete realization of your wish. It will come in a way that is so surprising and unbelievable, you'll know only a higher power could have done that. You'll be saying things like: "Wow, if I had wanted to do it this way, it wouldn't have ever worked!" It will look like a miracle. And it will be a miracle.

In any case, to reach that level of manifesting once you've decided to materialize a desire, you need to work toward it every day. It is fueled by your passion until it appears in your reality. It is something you cannot push aside without feeling as if something is missing. Usually, a *true* desire cannot go unfulfilled...that doesn't mean it will come into being on its own. As I said, if you don't work toward it, it will pile up, and in the meantime, you'll feel that hole in your heart getting bigger and bigger, until finally you realize all these unfulfilled desires are the root cause of your uneasiness in your life—then you'll start putting in the work!

The good news is that you do have a "savings" account, so nothing is ever lost in the Universe…only transformed! So don't wait any longer and start accepting the power you were born with.

CONCLUSION

As I am flying a few thousand feet above the ground, I am blinded by a bright light I haven't seen for a few weeks—the sun. I'm surrounded by clouds, and I feel a deep joy in my heart…witnessing this beauty from above is yet another testimonial to the fantastic power of manifesting from our thoughts into our world of physical form, because all this must have been thought of first!

After reading all the wonderful chapters from my co-manifestors, something struck a chord with me, and I hope with you as well. Through sharing their experiences with us, most of them described how they had hit a very challenging point in their lives. Almost all of them stated that the trigger to the change that took place was initiated by reaching a point of no return…accident, family issues, serious disease, you name it—struggles of all different kinds. Do we really need to hit rock bottom or have no other choice to be able to manifest the change our soul is craving? Or can we initiate the same outcome from a place of joy, satisfaction, and happiness? The answer to this question is included in the question itself—why would you look for change, for something new, whatever that may be, if you are already in a place of contentment? The only way for us to recognize and see the light is when it is contrasted with darkness—happiness with sorrow, success with frustration, and riches with poverty. So, yes, I do believe we cannot really expect or make an effort to manifest anything if a pre-condition does not trigger it.

We have all shared with you various testimonials to manifestation, and even if our desires were not always the same, we did share similarities in the way we materialized them. Peace of mind, internal work, meditation, firm decisions—no way out, only one possibility, which was going in and answering a call way bigger than any of us. All these are different kinds of indicators to a manifestation power at play.

Life is such a wonderful teacher. When you actually ask for something to come into your reality, when you decide what you want to manifest in your life, be ready, because that manifestation doesn't come without a price tag. The price is usually a test in disguise, a tsunami, which blasts through to rock and roll your world in a drastic way. It is a test in the sense that it gives you a chance for confirmation that you really want to manifest what you asked for—or not. If you give up because the test that comes beforehand is too hard, that only means you didn't really want it in the first place. It is also a preparation in the sense that to be able to handle what is to come, you must be ready, you must have the mindset and skills to welcome it in and keep it. So, yes, these big waves we have to surf before achieving our deep desires are a tough lesson to learn—but a necessary one.

What also transpired from all these chapters is the ease with which it all unfolded for most of the authors—ease once they had made a firm decision, that is. I remember how it felt for me. In retrospect, I can say the most difficult part was to actually make the decision in the first place.

I do hope this book has delivered on its promise. My goal was to give you hope, to inspire every single one of you to realize that manifesting your deep desires is not the panacea of a few privileged people but a birthright given to every soul taking on a human form, starting the moment we're conceived. This power is ours—it never left us. We just forgot about it, and when we do remember, we still don't have a clue how to use it. Now it is time to recover our memory and rediscover what we always knew how to use. This is not magic or some obscure faculty only possessed by a few initiated into the occult. There is nothing dark or sinister about this power; it is simply that—*power*. What you do with it could be considered as black or white, good or bad…it's entirely up to you.

I'm writing this conclusion while sitting in the plane—on my way to Cancun. This is another manifestation for me. I remember the pyramids standing stunningly in the middle of my dream board…now I'm realizing this is the last dream I'd manifested. My dream board is eighteen months old, so it's about time to upgrade it and focus on manifesting a brand new set of desires.

There is no limit, expiration date, or maximum timeline in terms of manifestation—you can manifest ANYTHING at any time. There is nothing too small or too big for the Universe. The only requirement is you must want it badly enough to materialize it. The more "obsessed" you are with your dream, the faster it gets delivered. So don't limit yourself...limitation is not a term that belongs in the Universe's dictionary. It's a human constraint created to justify our shortcomings and our fear of asking for what we really want.

Throughout the pages you have just read, just test and try what resonated the most with you, and then course correct. Create your own manifesting routine. You have the power to create the life you really want deep down and it starts right here!

DO YOU DREAM
OF BEING PUBLISHED?

What I enjoy most about my business is being able to collaborate with so many different women all over the world. But the best part is when I get to help them organize their very own collaborative work in an anthology book. That's where my real talent lies.

Without doubt, a book is THE asset to have to increase your visibility tenfold, to increase your clientele, and to gain instant credibility.

If you want to turn your dream of publishing your own anthology book into reality, get in touch with me and I'll show you how, together, we can accomplish this in ninety days, cost-free...and how you can actually make money right from the very start.

Sound good?

Then email me at christine@coachingandsuccess.com

Have a wonderful and successful life!

Christine Marmoy

THE END!